Graduate Job Hunting

on the internet

A practical illustrated guide
for all university and college leavers

Laurel Alexander
MCIPD MICG

www.internet-handbooks.co.uk

Other Internet Handbooks by the same author

Careers Guidance on the Internet
Education & Training on the Internet
Human Resource Management on the Internet
Overseas Job Hunting on the Internet
Working from Home on the Internet

© Copyright 2001 by Laurel Alexander

First published in 2001 by Internet Handbooks Ltd, Plymbridge House, Estover Road, Plymouth PL6 7PY, United Kingdom.

Customer services tel:	(01752) 202301
Orders fax:	(01752) 202333
Customer services email:	cservs@plymbridge.com
Distributors web site:	www.plymbridge.com
Internet Handbooks web site:	www.internet-handbooks.co.uk

Laurel Alexander has asserted her moral right to be identified as the author of this work.

Note: The contents of this book are offered for the purposes of general guidance only and no liability can be accepted for any loss or expense incurred as a result of relying in particular circumstances on statements made in this book. Readers are advised to check the current position with the appropriate authorities before entering into personal arrangements.

Case studies in this book are entirely fictional and any resemblance to real persons or organisations is entirely coincidental.

Typeset by PDQ Typesetting, Newcastle Under Lyme
Printed and bound by The Cromwell Press Ltd, Trowbridge, Wiltshire.

Graduate Job Hunting on the Internet

A practical illustrated guide for all university and college leavers

Internet Handbooks

Other titles in preparation

Contents

Contents

List of illustrations

Illustrations..

Preface

You've finally graduated from university, and been awarded that precious degree. What next?

The internet has opened up amazing opportunities for making a living. You can now easily search for work in any occupation and in any country. You can also bid for profitable work as a freelancer or contractor. You can have well-paid opportunities emailed to your desktop every day, you can apply for work overseas at the click of a button, and you can search databases containing thousands of vacancies whenever you like. Sites are tumbling out of the internet offering CV advice, career management skills, occupational information, and interview tips. You might even fancy setting up your own web site where you can advertise your skills, knowledge and expertise to prospective employers or clients.

In today's transient and unpredictable world of work, all of us – at every level and in every walk of life – need to constantly upgrade our skills and knowledge. Once again, the internet comes into its own. You can explore a huge number of distance learning courses and on-line learning opportunities on every conceivable topic.

One of the most valuable career management skills you can develop is networking. Indeed, effective networking is how successful people obtain most of their work. Again, the internet is one of the most powerful networking tools you can use, so make sure you are up to speed with your competitors.

In case you experience a problem accessing a particular web page, here are some tips to help you. First, make certain you have entered the URL correctly, since there is no room for error in the spelling either of words or of special characters. Next, try to access the site again later, as even the most visited sites are sometimes temporarily closed for maintenance. If that doesn't work, strip the URL back to its root address (in case the site's individual web pages have been reorganised) and try again. For example:

http://www.sitename.com/folder/page.html

http://www.sitename.com

Finally, the site may have moved to a new URL, without leaving a forwarding link. If so, try using one of the search engines mentioned in chapter 2 of this book. If that fails too, the site may for some reason have been withdrawn from service. In this case the search engine may suggest some useful alternatives.

I am grateful for all the help I have received from people in the course of researching and writing this book. All the web sites shown in this book remain the copyright of their respective owners. The screen shots of web sites were correct at the time of going to press and may appear different at different times. All trademarks and registered trademarks mentioned in this book are the property of their respective owners.

Finally, as a professional assessor and guidance specialist, I have had the pleasure and privilege over the years of helping many people make their successful transition into the workplace. I hope that, among all the information and hundreds of links contained in this book, you will find what you need to succeed on your path as a job hunter. Good luck!

Laurel Alexander
laurelalexander@internet-handbooks.co.uk

1 Graduate job hunting in the digital age

In this chapter we will explore:

► *the graduate employment scene*
► *flexible ways of working*
► *researching the job market*
► *creating your CV*
► *career networking*
► *applying for work*
► *attending interviews and meetings*
► *attending assessment centres*
► *taking psychometric tests*
► *applying for jobs online*
► *Financing postgraduate study*

. . . .

The graduate employment scene

The new millennium offers fantastic work opportunities to almost every-one, and as a new graduate about to enter the workplace, you have the pick of the best. Did you know:

(a) Only a minority of graduates enter traditional 'graduate jobs'.

(b) Graduates are expected to have 4 to 6 career changes in their working lives.

(c) Employment is global. People consider Europe and worldwide as well as Britain for work.

(d) Portfolio careers are developing, based on lots of diverse ways of earning money, not just from one employer.

Here are five tips for success in the changing employment world:

1. Think of employers as customers for your skills

2. Expect change, be ready for it and plan for it.

3. Gain as much technological experience as possible.

4. Develop a specialism, while being prepared to work as a generalist.

5. Be ready to build and use contacts.

Graduate job hunting in the digital age...............................

Grad facts

1. 25 per cent of employers expect a shortfall in recruitment this year.

2. On average 67.7 per cent of people apply for every graduate vacancy.

3. The average graduate employer handles around 4,000 applications.

4. Graduate salaries are predicted to grow by 5.5 per cent this year to a median figure of £17,400.

5. The top 10 per cent of employers pay around £21,000. The bottom 10 per cent pay around £15,400.

6. The skills most highly regarded by employers are: team working, interpersonal skills, motivation and enthusiasm.

7. The internet is being increasingly used for graduate recruitment. 44 per cent of graduate employers use it to promote specific vacancies and 21 per cent are planning to use it.

8. 66 per cent of graduates use the internet when looking for a job and 87 per cent say it will play an important role in graduate recruitment.

9. 66 per cent of final year students viewed corporate web sites for information on careers.

10. Sponsorship is on the rise. The number of sponsored students as a percentage of recruits grew by 15 per cent last year.

Flexible ways of working

Other than working in a full-time permanent position for an employer, you have other options in your choice of how you want to work. These include:

Teleworking
It is possible to have a regular job, get paid for it and stay at home to do it. Many large companies operate teleworking schemes whereby employees make use of technology and telecommunications from home. Or you could become a freelance teleworker based at home.

Franchises
A franchise gives you the right to sell an established company's goods or services in a particular geographical area.

Contract work
This type of work is becoming more commonplace. A contract differs from temporary work in that it is usually longer term and offers more benefits.

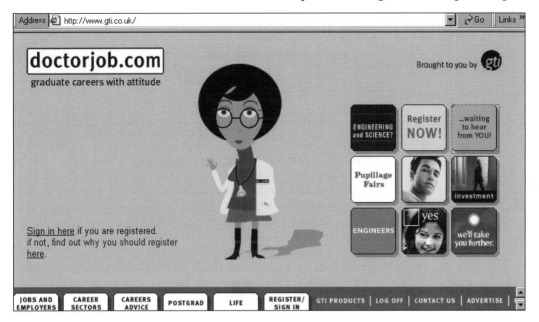

Working abroad
Members of the European Community (EC) have the right to live and work in other member states (including Belgium, Denmark, Greece, Republic of Ireland, France, Germany, Italy, Luxembourg, Netherlands, Spain and Portugal) without a work permit.

▶ *Key point* – UK nationals working in another member state have the same rights as nationals of that country with regard to salary, working conditions, training, social security and housing.

The Overseas Placing Unit (OPU) is a division of the government's Employment Service and can be contacted through any local Jobcentre. The OPU has access to overseas vacancies held on the national vacancy system and on the Oracle Jobfinder system. If you wish to find work outside the EC, the OPU can give advice but there is no current system for exchange of applications between the UK and other countries. Such vacancies are handled by commercial recruitment agencies.

Self-employment
Being self-employed is an option well worth considering if you like to be in control, enjoy a challenge and have a good idea to fill a niche in the market place.

Researching the job market

It is useful to consider the economic trends both nationally and locally when researching the job market. Issues such as the recession and the impact of local and national government budgets within your locality may affect the economic flow and therefore your employment. Your

Fig. 1. Doctor Job is for 'graduate careers with attitude.' It will email you details of jobs, employers, courses and news in your chosen careers sectors.

Graduate job hunting in the digital age......................................

local chamber of commerce, the town hall and Jobcentres could provide the information you require.

Be aware of the developmental progress of individual companies in your specialism or catchment area. Which new companies are moving in? Are any established companies considering expansion?

Applied technology is a booming market – computers, media, robotics, and virtual reality. All these are steadily growing areas. You need to be aware of the development of technology in your field of expertise. Will employment opportunities dwindle – or be changed in some way – as technology entrenches itself further? Do you want to be involved in that technology?

Are you aware of the demand rate for your area of expertise? Do you have your finger on the pulse, and a head start regarding new trends within your chosen profession?

Organising your jobsearch strategy

You will need to decide a number of key things: what skills you want to use, at what level you want to work, in what market you want to work, in what geographical area you want to work, and the salary you require. All this may seem pretty obvious, but it is amazing how many individuals launch themselves on the jobmarket, armed with a university degree but with no real jobsearch strategy in mind.

In your planning, you might want to use:

▶ *TECs (Training and Enterprise Councils)* – They provide funding and access to a broad range of services.

▶ *Registers and placement agencies* – In general, these tend to cater for junior, professional and lower management. Some agencies cater for more specific requirements such as accountancy. Charges are made to the employer and not to yourself. Be aware of being asked for money in lieu of work. This is unethical.

▶ *Careers Office* – There are career centres in most large towns and they provide information on local employment opportunities, career descriptions, information on what skills are needed for a particular job, information on training and educational opportunities.

▶ *Reference library* – The reference part of any library is an invaluable source of information. They usually have the national and local papers for reference as well as trade directories for researching company profiles. You can access contact names, addresses and telephone numbers. There is usually a photocopier available for use.

Researching a prospective employer

You can access the latest accounts and other financial information plus director names from the Registrar of Companies and Limited Partnerships. Your local chamber of commerce may also be able to help.

Creating your CV

Your CV is your sales brochure – selling you to prospective employees. It should be no longer than 2 pages and word-processed on light coloured, quality paper. You should customise your CV for each vacancy you are applying for. In the first quarter of the first page, include 2 or 3 separate sections detailing an area of expertise relevant to the work you are applying for. Within each section detail your accomplishments and abilities. State your degree or other qualifications near the top of your CV.

What to include in your CV

1. Full name.

2. Your full postal address and postcode.

3. Your telephone number and STD code and email address if you have one.

4. Key skills and experience (although this refers traditionally to paid work, consider unpaid work skills and knowledge and the skills and qualities you have gained through being a student).

5. Your secondary education with a summary of exams passed. If you are over 25, leave this out and focus on vocational/academic qualifications.

6. Further and higher education – college or university with exams/degree details.

7. Professional training – where and when with details of qualifications gained.

8. Employment history. Include your work experience, placements, and holiday work. For any gaps in your employment history put down the years rather than specific months and put details of things like 'unemployed but working in a voluntary capacity' or 'unemployed but took a course in learning German'.

9. Hobbies. Make these relevant to the position you are seeking without bending the truth too much. Add club membership or any positions of responsibility you have had as part of your interests.

10. Other information may include possession of a driving licence, knowledge of languages, community activities, whether you are a smoker or non-smoker, and whether you are able to work unsociable hours.

11. Your date of birth.

12. Two references. Your referees should be one or other of these: a teacher, tutor, minister, doctor, youth worker, previous employer, or a professionally qualified person.

You will need to develop portfolio of CVs, each targeted for specific areas of work. You also need to bear in mind that your CV will be sent by various methods, ranging from email to snail mail.

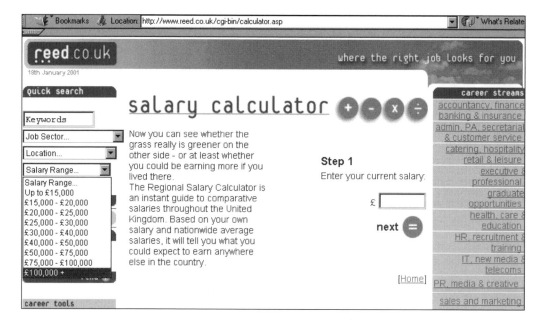

Fig. 2. The Reed web site is an excellent example of one with many useful features for job hunters, including this salary calculator.

Career networking

It has often been said that it's not what you know, but who you know, that matters. The right information, the best resources and the strongest support is needed to keep us focused in our jobsearch strategy. Ask yourself what are your career goals for the next six to twelve months – what do you need to achieve them, and who can help you achieve them?

Tips for successful career networking
1. Never ask for a job – ask for information.
2. Keep in touch with your contact.
3. Keep your contacts short and well spaced out in time.
4. Respect the limits of confidentiality.
5. Take as active a part as you can in any institutions or clubs that you belong to.
6. Be assertive without being aggressive.
7. Ask the right questions.
8. Use effective image and presentation skills.
9. Try to encourage people to think of you as knowledgeable or skilful.
10. Network by telephone.
11. Attend meetings and conferences.
12. Write letters.
13. When approaching companies with speculative letters, first identify the decision maker, and make it clear that you will be following up your inquiry.

Applying for work

When you telephone a company, either in response to an advert or on spec, your chances of selling yourself will depend on how your character and enthusiasm come across in your voice. Speak firmly, clearly and in a lively and enthusiastic manner – smiling helps. Don't suppress your body language. Try standing up while on the phone if you want to feel more confident and authoritative. Listen with your right ear to absorb facts, and your left ear for extra intuition. Listen to the tone and pitch of the other person's voice to try and detect any hidden meaning.

Covering letters

A covering letter is used when sending off your CV or an application form for a specifically advertised vacancy. Pointers to bear in mind:

1. Put your full address and telephone number in the letter, plus email address if you have one.

2. Ideally address your letter to a named person if stated in the advert. If there is no name address the letter, 'Dear Sir/Madam'.

3. If you address the letter to a named person, sign off 'Yours sincerely'. If you address the letter 'Dear Sir/Madam', you should sign off 'Yours faithfully'.

4. The first paragraph of the letters should state what you are replying to and where and when the advertisement or other information was seen.

5. The second paragraph should consist of your sales pitch, summarising your relevant skills, strengths and experience.

6. The third paragraph is where you should indicate your availability for interview, and say that you have enclosed your CV.

7. Whenever you put something else in an envelope other than the letter itself, always put Enc. (short for Enclosure) at the bottom left-hand corner of your letter.

Speculative letters

Speculative letters are a form of cold calling. They are written to companies with the intention of finding work, without directly asking for a job. There are four good reasons for writing speculative letters.

(a) When replying to an advertised vacancy, you may be one of fifty applicants. When you write a spec letter, you may be one of only two or three people doing the same thing.

(b) Your spec letter may arrive when a vacancy needs filling but is not yet advertised. Indeed, only a very small percentage of vacancies are filled by advertising.

(c) Your spec letter is likely to show initiative. It could be placed on file for the next suitable vacancy to arise.

(d) You are so good at selling yourself that you create a demand for your services.

Graduate job hunting in the digital age ....

A speculative letter is a business proposition and the aim is to get a meeting. With this in view, you need to customise each letter. Carefully research the organisation, targeting the letter at a named individual, and identifying where you might fit in. The first paragraph of the letter should state who you are, what you do and why you are writing. The second paragraph is your sales pitch containing relevant skills, strengths and experience. The third paragraph is where you request a meeting and indicate the enclosed résumé.

Press advertisements
It isn't usually advisable to place an advertisement for your services unless you are self-employed or looking to invest capital. It would be very unusual for a prospective employer to reply. If you are looking for employment, you could consider the national and local press, professional and trade journals.

Reading between the lines of a press vacancy
When applying via an advertisement for vacancies, you need to read the job description carefully for both the stated and hidden requirements. The obvious is down there in black and white – for example, well-motivated graduate required, or applicant must be prepared to travel throughout the UK. But it is the skills, knowledge and personal qualities not stated in the advertisement that are more likely to win you that interview. Pick out the subtle as well as the obvious requirements and you could position yourself ahead of the competition.

Attending interviews and meetings

An interview or a business meeting is your real chance to sell yourself. Did you know:

1. 55 per cent of your success will depend upon visual factors.

2. 38 per cent of your success will depend upon your voice.

3. 7 per cent of your success will depend upon your spoken word.

▶ *Key point* – Your success or otherwise will be determined within the first three minutes of your entering the room.

Positive body language
Sitting forward.
Nodding.
Direct eye contact.
Asking questions.
Interjecting with supportive comments.
Using non-threatening gestures.
Initiating and maintaining conversation.
Being polite and courteous.

Smiling.
Sitting with open, unfolded arms and legs.
Keeping an upright body.
Even and deep breathing.

Positive speech patterns
Showing sincerity.
Being controlled and fluent.
Making suggestions.
Remaining brief and to the point.
Using questions.
Making constructive use of the 'I' word.
Offering constructive criticism.
Using expressions such as: Let's… Suppose we… What about… How can we resolve this?

Dress and appearance
Even the colours you wear convey certain impressions to those you are with. Did you know:

1. Red suggests that a person is confident, energised, outgoing and authoritative.

2. Green suggests that a person is dependable, security-minded, calming and self-reliant.

3. Blue suggests that a person is trustworthy, calm, intuitive and confident.

4. Yellow suggests that a person is successful, active, logical, open minded, constructive and cheerful.

5. Orange suggests that a person is enthusiastic, assertive and creative.

The interview
The interview is your opportunity to sell yourself directly to a company. You will be asked questions and maybe given tasks to do. Answer the questions as fully as you can without waffling. Think of the answers that they are likely to be looking for and provide them together with examples of your related skills and knowledge. Show them by illustration what you can do and what you know. And remember, you have as much right to ask questions of any prospective employer as they do of you.

Your successful interview checklist
1. Research the company and be sure you know what the position is all about.

2. Ask some intelligent and relevant questions.

3. Be enthusiastic without going overboard.

4. Shake hands on entering and on leaving.

5. Looking the interviewer/panel in the eye with a smile.

6. Sit upright and relaxed in the chair.

7. Think professionally – behave professionally.

Handling second interviews
Second interviews vary a good deal. Sometimes they are simply a repeat of the first interview or they may last a full day and involve various selection methods. There are several possible selection methods, some of which are outlined in the next section.

Attending assessment centres

Increasingly, firms like to take potential recruits away for a few days so that they can reach more informed decisions about who to hire. The belief is that employers can gain more information on candidates' abilities with respect to key job demands. An interview is sometimes seen more as a self report, not backed up by evidence of the applicant's ability to perform. Surveys reveal that over one third of the Times Top 1000 companies use assessment centres today.

The assessment process
The process will generally involve:

(a) Several candidates being observed together.

(b) A number of assessors or observers being present.

(c) A range of assessment techniques – to measure the candidates in different ways.

(d) Assessment on a number of dimensions e.g. leadership skills.

(e) A consensus hire decision.

More and more companies are placing an emphasis on interpersonal skills (people skills). Candidates will find their behavioural skills put to the test to see how well they work with others and how well they communicate. The main groups of attributes that are sought by employers, and tested at assessment centres, are:

1. Relationships – teamwork, interpersonal skills, oral communication.

2. Action – leadership, motivation, flexibility.

3. Presence – self-confidence, calmness, political awareness, communication skills.

4. Judgement – analytical reasoning, decision-making, commercial awareness, strategic planning.

Typically assessment centres are comprised of group discussions, personality tests, ability tests, presentation skills, team tasks and role-plays. Equally these methods of assessment could be used during an interview.

Written exercises
You will have a set time to read background material and write something. For example you might be asked to draft a letter on a given topic.

Or you might be asked to work through papers dealing with a complex problem and write a report summarising the facts, outlining alternative solutions, and making your own recommendation on the best one. The selectors are testing your analytical powers and whether you can express complex ideas in a clear, concise and tactful way.

Role play
Think about what the assessors are looking for. Often the role will deliberately place you in a difficult or confrontational situation to see how well you handle it.

Group discussions
Most jobs involve working in teams. The employer will naturally be interested in how you get on with colleagues, subordinates, and people senior to you. At the second interview you are likely to be brought together with some of your fellow candidates and asked to work together on a group activity. For example you might be asked to discuss a topic with your fellow candidates. or to analyse information and reach a conclusion.

Whatever the task, the recruiter is looking out for how you interact with other people. Can you bring out the best in them when you are asked to take the lead? Can you be genuinely supportive when someone else is in charge? These issues, of being a good team member and, particularly, of being a good team leader, are usually far more important to the selectors than whether or not you successfully complete the task you have been set. You want to come across as someone who is aware of others and able to work well with them.

In-tray exercises
These are designed to simulate the administrative aspects of a job. You might be asked to deal with a range of items and the most important thing for you to do is to prioritise and then do the tasks. These tests measure your ability to prioritise and act effectively under pressure.

Giving presentations
You have to make a brief presentation to the selectors and your fellow candidates. You might be given a list of topics and have to choose one. The selectors are looking for whether you can communicate well with an audience.

Team exercises
These may involve being asked to construct something practical and are aimed at identifying action attributes such as leadership, motivation and creativity.

Taking psychometric tests

Psychometric tests are often used by employers as one of their selection methods. Such tests are endorsed by the British Psychological Society and administered by a qualified person. The objectives of the tests are to further affirm your suitability for a post. The questionnaires are concerned

Graduate job hunting in the digital age...........................

Fig. 3. From a web site like this, you can use the internet to gain some practice with personality testing.

with your typical or preferred ways of behaving – the way you relate to others or approach problems. When used with other methods it is believed that they can explore how well you are suited to a particular job. Employers may use these tests at various points in their selection process.

Aptitude tests
These are multiple-choice questions, administered under exam conditions with strict time limits. They are designed to assess your powers of
logical reasoning. They have clear right and wrong answers. There are
lots of different types, but typically one part will measure verbal reasoning, another numerical reasoning, and perhaps a third will measure spatial
or diagrammatic reasoning. To obtain a good score you have to do better
than the 'norm group', which is likely to be people successfully doing the
job you are applying for. You won't know what the standard is, but a
rough rule of thumb might be that you should aim to complete 70 to 80
per cent of the questions, and get most of them (70 to 80 per cent) right.
Some tips:

1. At the start of the test, quickly work out how much time you have for
    each question. Keep aware of the time as you work through the ques-
    tions.

2. If you get stuck on a question, don't spend too long on it, but move on
    to the next one. However, don't abandon a question prematurely, if
    with a few extra seconds you might have solved it. You have to get
    the balance right and achieve a rhythm where you don't get bogged
    down. On the other hand don't skim over questions in too superficial
    a way.

3. If you aren't sure of an answer, bear in mind that you won't have time
    to come back to it later, so put down your best guess and move on.

4. The test will have some practice questions at the start. Make sure you
    understand these thoroughly before the test itself begins.

5. Finally, try not to be overawed by the formal nature of the test, or to be
    panicked by the time pressure.

Completing personality questionnaires

These are used to see how you react to different situations. They measure a variety of personal qualities, usually characteristics such as how determined you are and your social skills. The questionnaires are usually untimed, but you will be asked to put down your first reaction to the questions and not spend time pondering their meaning. Some tips:

▶ Many employers want candidates with a balance of different personal qualities: for example, being able to get on with people, take charge and organise, be persistent and determined.

▶ The particular requirements of the job you are applying for might give a clue to the qualities the employer seeks. For example, a sales job may look for people who enjoy meeting new people, while a job where you have to analyse information may favour those who like paying attention to detail.

Applying for jobs online

Electronic applications are those that employ any sort of computer method in the recruitment process. They might include the following:

1. You might be asked to apply directly to the organisation using email. Many organisations now offer the chance for you to 'post your CV on the web'. This means entering it into the database of an organisation that will either try actively to get you a job or will passively allow an employer to interrogate their database and select you for interview from your CV details.

2. Some companies ask you to put your application onto a diskette.

3. Other types of electronic methods of getting work involve Usenet newsgroups, some of which are dedicated to recruitment and may have names such as jobs.offered and jobs.wanted. You can send your details to such newsgroups or apply for posts you see advertised on them.

4. You might send a paper CV to a company that then uses optical character recognition (OCR) software to scan it into the computer database.

5. You may decide to publish your own web site on the internet, to present information about yourself and your CV.

Filling in forms on screen

Some employers and recruitment agencies enable you to apply for jobs by completing an on-screen form. Employers and agencies may use standard searches to find candidates. These often rely on finding specific key words in the descriptions of your various activities so make sure you use positive, active words that are appropriate to the type of work for which you are applying.

Graduate job hunting in the digital age ....

Writing CVs

Sample CVs

Online CVs

Posting CVs

Follow up

Sending your CV by email

You could send your CV as a formatted document in an attachment to your email message. However, you may run the risk of their email system not being able to handle your attachment. You need to send your application in a format which can be read by any computer, and this means using ASCII code (American Standard Code for Information Interchange). If you were to send it as an email attachment in Microsoft Word, the receiving company's computer might translate it automatically into a garbled mess. You can type it into your word processor rather than use the text message part of your email tool, but if you do, you need to remember the following:

1. Use a standard monospaced font such as Courier. Other proportionally spaced fonts change accordingly when you convert them and alter any tab settings you have used creating a mess. You cannot use bold or italic type in ASCII.

2. You cannot use special indents or margin adjustments, although you can use ordinary tabs and spacing.

3. Keep individual lines to less than 70 characters wide. The receiving computer may have different screen widths and email tools which will create a garbled mess out of anything wider than 70 characters. You can create some interest in the document by using hyphens, asterisks and the letter 'o' for bullet points.

4. Save your file in ASCII by opening the File menu and using the Save As option. Name your file and save it as a Text Only file if you are using Word.

5. You can send it as an attachment in your email by specifying the directory (folder) it is in on your hard drive. Or, you can paste it into the text message area and send it as you would a normal email message.

If you want to email your CV, clarify whether you need to send the CV in the main body of the text or as an attachment. Bear in mind when sending your CV in the main body of an email what your viewer will see first on their screen. Start your CV with a career summary or employment objective and put contact details at the end. Don't forget to send a covering letter, just as you would in print, unless you are instructed not to do so by the receiving organisation.

Posting CVs

You can also post your CV to one of the jobs.wanted newsgroups or the misc.jobs.resumes newsgroups. The former tends to be related to an area of work and the latter covers any work and any country. A recent *Tomorrow's World* on BBC television suggested that around 15 major companies are now using this method in the UK. It is far more common in the USA and observers believe that it will grow in popularity here.

When posting a CV to a CV bank or employment agency database, you need to be clear about the kind of work you are looking for. A CV format will have to be completed that is the same for everyone. Employers will use key words to select CVs they want to examine further.

Scanning CVs
If you are preparing a CV for scanning with OCR software, bear in mind the following:

1. Don't use unusual or stylised fonts in paper CVs that may potentially be scanned. Use a standard and traditional font such as Arial or Times New Roman in 12 point.

2. Use a font size of 10 point or greater.

3. Use white or very light paper. Scanners do not pick up well from coloured paper.

4. Don't fold your CV. Send it in a full-sized A4 envelope. Folded paper sometimes does not scan well.

5. Place your name on its own at the top of each page.

6. Do not use bullets, bold, italics, underlining or graphics.

7. Provide a laser-printed original copy.

8. Do not staple sheets together.

9. Save your word-processed CV as a plain text or ASCII file.

Employers who use automated CV selection are often using scanning software programmed to search for words reflecting key skills including industry jargon. You need to elaborate and specify your key words. Note that especially in the IT field, skills such as Unix or network management may be specifically searched for. So include everything you think may be relevant to the post for which you are applying.

Fig. 4. Submitting a CV at the Jobsearch web site.

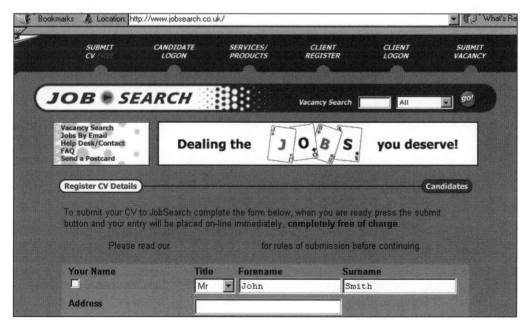

Graduate job hunting in the digital age....................................

Creating CVs
There are many internet resources for creating online CVs. One of the best ones is:

http://www.jobsearch.co.uk

This allows you to create CVs that can be accessed by UK employers using the JobSearch database. Another site worth visiting is:

http://www.monsterboard.com

My Monster
Free personal career a

Create your online CV
New jobs emailed to ye
Manage your personal

Career Centre
Articles on CVs, Intervi
Ask our Experts for ad
Visit Graduate and oth

This is a large and established source of vacancies. You are also able to access their CV Builder page to complete a pro forma CV or to submit your own. Note: some organisations charge a fee for their CV-building services.

Putting your CV on your own home page
This method may be useful for those who are hoping to get into the area of web page design and can demonstrate their skills.

Financing postgraduate study

With the exception of teacher training, funding for postgraduate research or courses (academic or vocational) isn't automatic. Your right to LEA funding will stop when your first degree ends. For very few courses is your LEA allowed to give you a further (discretionary) grant. For post-graduate study, the possible funding body depends on the subject, so find out which one deals with what you want to do. Here are some ways to get financial help:

▶ *Family support* – Help with fees, loans or accommodation.

▶ *Loans* – Postgraduates are not entitled to student loans but can apply for Career Development Loans: ring 0800 585505 for details. Some TECs (Training & Enterprise Councils) offer loan packages. Sometimes banks give loans for courses leading to professional qualifications in areas such as law and business.

▶ *Charities* – May provide small grants. The careers service and public libraries have directories of trusts and charities.

▶ *Research assistantships* – Often these offer the chance to register for a higher degree while you help an academic with his or her research (usually scientific). Assistantships are advertised in the *Times Higher Education Supplement* or *New Scientist*.

▶ *Scholarships* – There are a few scholarships and other awards, often reserved for applicants to particular universities. They are mostly for academic postgraduate study, not vocational courses.

▶ *Sponsorship* – Employers sometimes sponsor students for first degrees. You could ask employers if they would be willing to sponsor your postgraduate course, but they are likely to say yes only if the subject is directly relevant to them.

▶ *Doing your postgrad part time* – Many courses are available part time, in day, evening and distance learning formats. Fees are often cheaper than for full time study. If you are in work and want financial help from your employer you will probably have to establish yourself as a good employee first. If the course is less than 21 hours supervised study (including homework) you may be eligible for welfare benefits, but check with your local DSS office.

Main grant-giving bodies
There are a number of grant-giving bodies such as:

> Biotechnology and Biological Sciences Research Council.
>
> British Academy (for the humanities).
>
> Department for Education (for some taught courses of a vocational and professional nature such as librarianship).
>
> Economic and Social Research Council (for most social science subjects).
>
> Engineering and Physical Science Research Council.
>
> Local Education Authority: there is an automatic grant for teacher training.
>
> Ministry of Agriculture Fisheries and Food.
>
> Medical Research Council.
>
> Natural Environment Research Council.
>
> Particle Physics and Astronomy Research Council.

GENERAL INFORMATI
. . . .
Before submitting an ap
How to apply
Outline applications
Peer Review Guidelines
Case for Support
Timing and Award Decis
Publication of data
Standards of service
Institution Eligibility
Head Office contacts
Assessment procedures
Grant Terms and Condit

You don't apply direct to the research councils. However, you can approach them for advice if your subject is a borderline case and it isn't clear which of them might support it. To be eligible for an award, you have to be resident in the UK – not for the purposes of education – for three years before your postgraduate study begins. Different procedures may apply if you are from Scotland, Northern Ireland, the Isle of Man, or the Channel Islands. If you are a national from another country in the European Economic Area you usually can't apply for a full award, but you may be eligible for a fees award from a research council.

Finally…

The following chapters of this book cover the topics listed below, with key points of interest.

▶ Distance and online courses – details of international distance and open education and training as well as online courses.

▶ Vocational training – sites offering vocational training resources and courses.

▶ Industry-specific employment agencies – national and international employment agencies relating to specific occupations.

Graduate job hunting in the digital age ....

▶ Industry-specific careers & training information – national and international sites offering career and training data.

▶ Recruitment and vacancies – a wide selection of agencies offering access to thousands of jobs.

▶ Specialist graduate sites – several of these sections include graduate sites but these were picked for their specialist content.

▶ Employers – direct links into major employers' web sites.

▶ Careers guidance – sites offering information, CV production, interview tips and jobsearch strategies.

▶ Freelance and self-employment – a selection of sites offering opportunities and support to the self employed.

▶ Financial – grants, funding, loans and venture capital information.

▶ Telecommuting – details of sites offering telework opportunities and support.

▶ Research – information on various research sources including government, company research and benefits.

▶ Magazines, journals and newspapers – a selection of online press media offering vacancies and career information.

▶ Best of the rest – a selection of web sites covering everything from student support to management development, self assessments and voluntary work.

More Internet Handbooks to help you

Careers Guidance on the Internet, Laurel Alexander
Creating a Home Page on the Internet, Richard Cochrane
Discussion Forums on the Internet, Kye Valongo
Education & Training on the Internet, Laurel Alexander
Finding a Job on the Internet, Brendan Murphy (2nd edition)
Internet For Students, David Holland
Internet Skills for the Workplace, Ian Hosker
Overseas Job Hunting on the Internet, Laurel Alexander
Using Email on the Internet, Kye Valongo
Where to Find it on the Internet, Kye Valongo (2nd edition)

Visit the free Internet HelpZone at
www.internet-handbooks.co.uk
Helping you master the internet

---

2 Searching for information

In this chapter we will explore:

▶ *searching the internet*
▶ *tips for searching*
▶ *bookmarking your favourite web sites*
▶ *search engines and directories*
▶ *search utilities*
▶ *portal sites for graduate job hunters*
▶ *portal sites for newspapers and magazines*

. . . .

Searching the internet

The usual way to look up something on the internet is to go to the web site of a well-known search engine or internet directory. These services are free and open to everyone.

▶ *Search engines* – These are also known as spiders or crawlers. They have highly sophisticated search tools that automatically seek out web sites across the internet. These trawl through and index literally millions of pages of internet content. As a result they often find information that is not listed in traditional directories.

▶ *Internet directories* – These are developed and compiled by people, rather than by computers. Web authors submit their web site details, and these details get listed in the relevant sections of the directory.

The browser that your ISP supplies you with – typically Internet Explorer or Netscape – should include an internet seach facility, ready for you to use, but you are perfectly free to visit any of the search engines listed below, and use them yourself.

Most people refer to directories as search engines and lump the two together. For the purposes of this book, we will refer to them all as search engines. Popular search engines have now become big web sites in their own right, usually combining many useful features. As well as search boxes where you can type key words to summarise what you are looking for, you will usually also find handy directories of information, news, email and many other services. There are hundreds if not thousands of search engines freely available. The biggest and best known are AltaVista, Google, Excite, Infoseek, Lycos and Yahoo! (the most popular of all).

Tips for searching

1. If you want general information, try Yahoo! or AltaVista first. For specific information, try one or more of the major search engines. After experimenting, many people decide on their own favourite search engine and stick to it most of the time.

2. If you do a search for graduate vacancies the search engine will search for graduate and search for vacancies quite separately. This could produce details of graduate studies and hotel vacancies, for example. The way to avoid this is to enclose all your key words inside a pair of quotation marks. If you type in graduate vacancies– then only web sites with that combination of words should be listed for you.

3. George Boole was a 19th-century English mathematician who worked on logic. He gave his name to Boolean operators – simple words like AND, OR and NOT. If you include these words in your searches, it should narrow down the results, for example: 'careers AND law NOT America'. However, don't go overboard and restrict the search too much, or you may get few or no results.

4. Try out several different search engines, and see which one you like the best. Or you could obtain the handy little search utility called Web Ferret (see below): if the information is not on one search engine, Web Ferret can usually find it on one or more of the others.

Bookmarking your favourite web sites

Your browser (usually Internet Explorer or Netscape Navigator) enables you to save the addresses of any web sites you specially like and may want to revisit. These are called Bookmarks in Netscape, or Favorites in Internet Explorer (US spelling). In either case, simply mouse-click on the relevant button on your browser's toolbar – Bookmarks or Favorites as the case may be. This produces a drop-down menu that you click on to add the site concerned. When you want to revisit that site later, click again on the same button, then click the name of the web site you bookmarked, and within a few seconds it should open.

Search engines

AltaVista
http://www.altavista.com
http://www.altavista.co.uk
Alta Vista is one of the most popular search sites among web users worldwide. It contains details of millions of web pages on its massive and ever-growing database. You can either follow the trails of links from its home page, or (better) type in your own key words into its search box. You can even search in about 25 different languages. The dedicated UK page has a link to 'jobs', leading to additional links to IT and computers, job banks, job search, and working holidays. Of course, you can also do you own searches for specific information.

Ask Jeeves
http://www.askjeeves.com
Ask Jeeves offers a slightly different approach to searches. It invites you to ask questions on the internet just as you would of a friend or colleague. For example, you could type in something like: 'Where can I find out about graduate training?' Jeeves retrieves the information, drawing from a knowledge base of millions of standard answers.

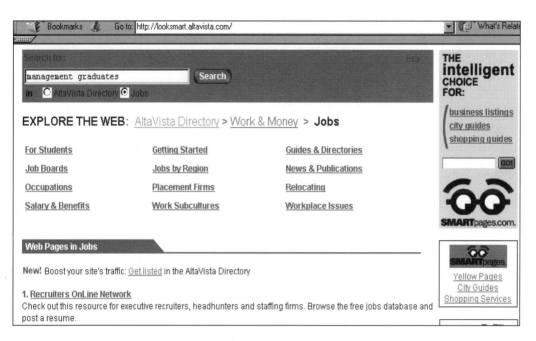

Electronic Yellow Pages
http://www.eyp.co.uk
These electronic yellow pages are organised on the same lines as the paper edition. Just type in the details of the information you need – anything from careers to training – and it quickly searches for appropriate services in your local area.

Fig. 5. Using the AltaVista search engine to explore opportunities for management graduates.

Excite
http://www.excite.com
http://www.excite.co.uk
Excite is another of the top ten search engines and directories on the internet. To refine your search, simply click the check boxes next to the words you want to add and then click the Search Again button. There are separate Excite home pages for several different countries and cultures including Australia, Chinese, France, German, Italy, Japan, Netherlands, Spain, Sweden, and the USA. Excite, too, now has a substantial UK section, and the home page contains a link 'Find a job'. You can do company search, and explore jobhunting tips. Also, try typing in 'graduate recruitment' into the search box.

Global Online Directory
http://www.god.co.uk
Launched in 1996, GOD is fairly unusual among search engines in that it is UK based, and aims to be a premier European search service. Features of the site include a 'global search' where you can search for web sites by country, state, province, county or even city by city, narrowing down the information for a more focused result.

Searching for information..

Google

http://www.google.com

A new and innovative search site is Google, which has an easy-to-use no-nonsense format. It matches your query to the text in its index, to find relevant pages. For instance, when analysing a page for indexing, it looks at what the pages linking to that page have to say about it, so the rating partly depends on what others say about it. This highly regarded search facility has indexed well over a billion pages on the world wide web, and is now helping to power Yahoo!

HotBot Jobs

http://www.hotbot.com/jobs

This is an impressive, very popular, and well-classified search engine and directory, now associated with Lycos. From this page you can link to CareerBuilder, careers pages and portals.

Infoseek

http://www.infoseek.co.uk

Through the UK home page of this popular search engine you can access links to work, training, CV posting, vacancies, advice and recruitment agencies.

Internet Address Finder

http://www.iaf.net

The IAF is used by millions of web users for searching and finding the names, email addresses, and now Intel Internet videophone contacts, of other users worldwide. With millions of addresses it is one of the most comprehensive email directories on the internet. By registering, you will also enable others to find you.

Internet Public Library

http://www.ipl.org/ref/

The IPL runs an experimental 'Ask-a-Question' service. The librarians who work here are mostly volunteers with other full-time librarian jobs. Your question is received at the IPL Reference Centre and the mail is reviewed once a day and questions are forwarded to a place where all the librarians can see them and answer them.

List of Search Engines

http://www.search-engine-index.co.uk

This enterprising British site offers a free list of hundreds of search engines, covering all kinds of different topics. There are software search engines, multiple search engines, email and news search engines, web search engines, commercial search engines, word reference and science search, law search, TV, film and music search, image search, technology manufacturers search, and various localised search engines.

Looksmart

http://www.looksmart.com

This is another good directory with a huge number of catalogued sites. You can find it on the Netscape Net Search Page. If your search is not successful, you are redirected to AltaVista.

Lycos
http://www.lycos.com
http://www.lycos.co.uk
Founded in 1995, Lycos is another of the top ten worldwide web search engines. Lycos is the name for a type of ground spider ('spider' being the term for a type of search engine). It searches document titles, headings, links and keywords and returns the first few words of each page it indexes for your search. Since 1997, with the media giant Bertelsmann, it has launched Lycos sites in 11 European countries.

Metacrawler
http://www.metacrawler.com/
MetaCrawler was originally developed by Erik Selberg and Oren Etzioni at the University of Washington, and released to the internet in 1995. In response to each user query, it incorporates results from all the top search engines. It collates results, eliminates duplication, scores the results and provides the user with a list of relevant sites.

SavvySearch
http://www.savvysearch.com/
Owned by CNET, SavvySearch is one of the leading providers of meta-search services. It offers a single point of access to hundreds of different search engines, guides, archives, libraries and other resources. You type in a keyword query which is then immediately sent out to all appropriate internet search engines. The results are gathered and displayed within a few seconds.

Scoot Yahoo!
http://scoot.yahoo.co.uk
Yahoo! has combined with the British directory Scoot to offer a search facility for people seeking UK-oriented information, businesses and organisations. Once you have found the organisation you are looking for, you can click straight into their web site if they have one.

Search.com
http://search.cnet.com
This service is run by CNET, one of the world's leading new-media companies. From the home page you can click an A-Z list of options which displays an archive of all its search engines. The list is long, but just about everything you need to master the web is there. You can search yellow pages, phone numbers, email addresses, message boards, software downloads, and easily do all kinds of special searches.

Search Engine Colossus
http://www.searchenginecolossus.com
Here you will find a huge collection of links to just about every search engine in the world.

Lycos Services
- Free SMS NEW
- £10k to be won NEW
- Free text messaging
- Free Email
- Weather
- Lycos Chat
- My Lycos
- Play Games Online
- UK Maps
- Free Internet Access
- Lycos Radio
- Free Home Page

Lycos Partner
- BT
- Loot
- Thomson Directories
- Travel@leisureplanet
- Books@BOL.com
- Mortgages with John C

Searching for information..

UK Directory
http://www.ukdirectory.co.uk
This is a useful directory listing to UK-based web sites. You can browse it or search it. It has a well-classified subject listing. UK Directory is simple and intuitive to use. You don't need to know the name of the company, service or person to find the things you are interested in. Just look in the category that best suits your needs. Use it like a telephone directory.

UK Plus
http://www.ukplus.co.uk
The parent company of this UK-oriented search engine and database is the Daily Mail & General Trust – owners of the *Daily Mail,* the *Mail on Sunday, London Evening Standard* and a number of UK regional news-papers – so it draws on a long tradition of publishing. It has built up a vast store of web site reviews written by a team of journalists. Although it concentrates on UK web sites, you will also find many from all over the world which are likely to be of interest to British-based readers.

UK Yellow Web Directory
http://www.yell.co.uk

Fig. 6. In addition to its main search page, the Yahoo! internet directory also maintains a special database called Yahoo! Employment, illustrated here.

This site is operated by the yellow pages division of British Telecom. It is indexed 'by humans' and is searchable. A number of non-UK sites are included in the database. There is also an A to Z company listing, but note that companies whose names begin with 'The' are listed under T. A Business Compass lists 'the best' business internet resources, with links and brief descriptions.

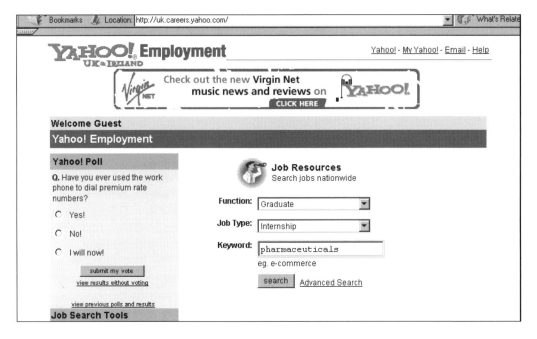

Webcrawler
http://webcrawler.com
Webcrawler is a fast worker and returns an impressive list of links. It analyses the full text of documents, allowing the searcher to locate key words which may have been buried deep within a document's text. Webcrawler is now part of Excite.

World Email Directory
http://www.worldemail.com
This site is dedicated to email, email, more email, finding people and locating businesses and organisations. WED has access to an estimated 18 million email addresses and more than 140 million business and phone addresses world wide. You will find everything from email software, to email list servers, global email databases, business, telephone and fax directories and a powerful email search engine.

Yahoo!
http://www.yahoo.com
http://www.yahoo.co.uk
Yahoo! was the first substantial internet directory, and continues to be one of the best for free general searching. It contains over a billion links categorised by subject. You can 'drill down' through the well-organised categories to find what you want, or you can carry out your own searches using keywords. The site also offers world news, sport, weather, email, chat, retailing facilities, clubs and many other features. Yahoo! is probably one of the search engines and directories you will use time after

Fig. 7. Using the search utility Web Ferret to search for opportunities for marketing graduates.

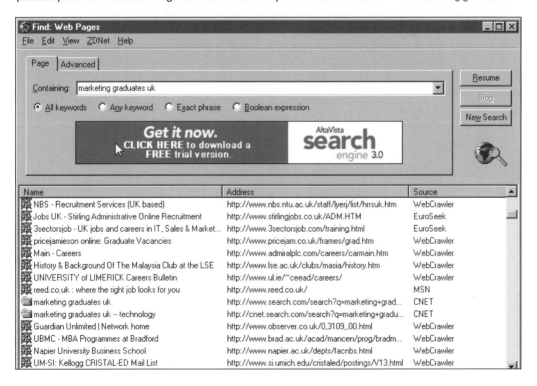

time, as do millions of people every day. Look for the link to Business and Economy. From there you can click onto Employment for thousands of links.

Search utilities

WebFerret
http://www.ferretsoft.com
WebFerret is an excellent functional search utility. You can key in your query offline, and when you connect it searches the web until it has collected all the references you have specified — up to 9,999 if you wish. WebFerret queries ten or more search engines simultaneously and discards any duplicate results. The search engines it queries include Alta-Vista, Yahoo, Infoseek, Excite, and others. You can immediately visit the web pages it lists for you, even while WebFerret is still running. The trial version of the program is free, and simplicity itself. It only takes a few minutes to download from FerretSoft. Highly recommended.

Portal sites for graduate job hunters

@Computer Weekly
http://www.computerweekly.co.uk/cw.home/cw.home.asp
This is an online version of magazine for UK info-tech professionals: news, features, careers, discussions, recommended books and e-mail forum. They also offer a free email jobs service.

AGCSI Graduate Careers Ireland
http://www.gradireland.com/
AGCSI aims to lead, support and develop collaboration among higher education careers services in the development and delivery of high quality careers guidance for students and graduates, and in their work with employers and academics. It seeks to be the leading source of expertise on career guidance and information on employment and training opportunities for higher education students and graduates in Ireland. There are some useful student links on the site.

Association of Graduate Careers Advisory Services
http://agcas.csu.ac.uk
All higher education institutions seek to develop the employability and career opportunities of their graduates. Institution-based careers advisory services play a vital role in this task. AGCAS promotes collaboration between its members to develop and deliver effective and high quality careers services. It represents over 1,100 careers staff in 130 higher education institutions throughout the UK and Eire.

Association of Graduate Recruiters
http://www.agr.org.uk
Established in 1968, the AGR represents organisations which recruit and employ graduates or which offer services in connection with graduate recruitment.

BT Change Jobs
http://www.changejobs.co.uk
Here you will find links to recruitment sites and information on how to go
about it. There is also an online job search, professional advice plus tips
for graduates.

Careers Guidance and Counselling
http://www.unn.ac.uk/academic/hswe/careers/index2.html
This is a huge site put together by the University of Northumbria. You can
explore 1,500 active links to relevant sites. The links cover the full range of
relevant academic disciplines – plus education, training and employment
links.

Career Guide
http://www.careerguide.net
The Career Guide is a resource directory of online career related service
providers for consumers and corporate visitors.

Career Resource Centre
http://www.careers.org
From the home page, you can link into US and Canadian jobs, employer
directories, learning resources, home office resources and career services.

Careers Gateway
http://www.careersoft.co.uk
With links to the web sites of professional bodies, universities and a host
of sites to help with job seeking, you could usefully start your career

Fig. 8. CareerGuide.

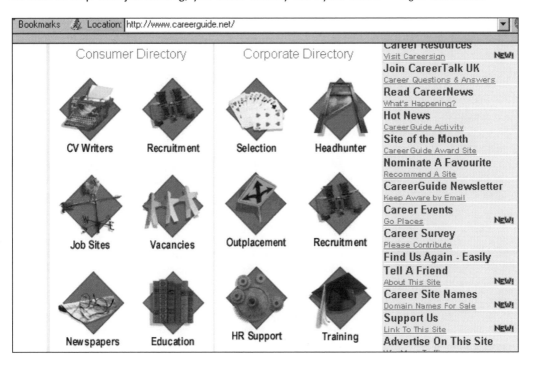

surfing here. Careers teachers and advisers will also find some helpful teaching ideas and resources.

Careers Portal
http://www.careers-portal.co.uk
Jobs, careers advice and services, universities, schools and colleges are all on this UK search directory.

Careers Information and Guidance on the Web
http://www.aiuto.net/uk.htm
This is a 60-page guide to over 400 British web sites dedicated to job search, the professions, vocational training, universities and research.

Department for Education and Employment
http://www.dfee.gov.uk
There is a search facility on the home page of this site where you can find documents relating to a particular topic. By clicking onto an alphabetical letter you can view a list of topics beginning with that letter. The links option brings up related sites such as the Teacher Training Agency.

DfEE Careers & Information Division Home Page
http://www.dfee.gov.uk/cid/index.htm
The division includes the Careers & Occupational Information Centre (COIC). The site contains information on: government policy on careers, education and guidance, what the Careers & Information Division does and the publications they produce.

Electronic Recruiting News
http://www.interbiznet.com
The particular focus of this US web site is to chronicle, analyse and report on the evolution of electronic recruiting. Over 5,000 pages link you to recruitment resources plus three online daily updates that cover many aspects of electronic recruiting.

Employment Index
http://www.employmentindex.com
There are four sections on the home page. You can explore employment topics, job seekers metalinks worldwide, and search engines.

Employment Service
http://www.employmentservice.gov.uk
The ES is the government agency responsible for helping the unemployed in England, Scotland and Wales to find work. Here they outline their services for jobseekers and employers looking to fill posts. Those out of work can check online for the latest vacancies.

Graduate Connection
http://www.graduateconnection.ac.uk
Graduate Connection aims to help small and medium sized companies make more use of the skills of West Midlands' students and graduates. It

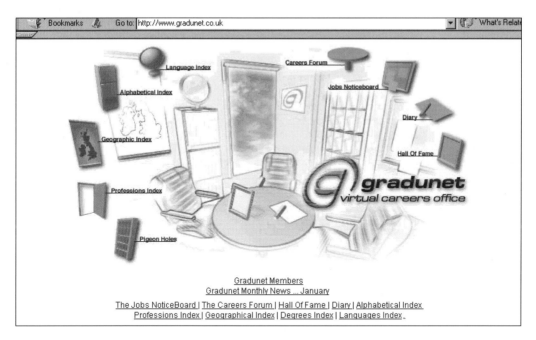

Gradunet Members
Gradunet Monthly News ... January
The Jobs NoticeBoard | The Careers Forum | Hall Of Fame | Diary | Alphabetical Index
Professions Index | Geographical Index | Degrees Index | Languages Index

is a consortium of universities, TECs, Chambers of Commerce and graduate links, sharing the idea that local students and graduates could be helping companies in this region to compete better, develop new ideas, introduce new technologies and contribute towards efficiency.

Fig. 9. The web site of Gradunet.

Gradunet
http://www.gradunet.co.uk
The site contains links to Gradunet Monthly News, a jobs noticeboard, careers forum, hall of fame, diary, alphabetical index, professions index, geographical index, degrees index, and languages index. You can click on your chosen profession to explore a list of companies offering vacancies, celebrity and graduate profiles, relevant links, professional bodies and more industry news.

GET: The Directory of Graduate Recruiters
http://www.get.hobsons.com
Hobsons are publishers of the GET directory. This is a very useful careers portal web site including careers and recruitment information. There are links to careers search, over 25,000 current vacancies for graduates, job descriptions, student services, careers guidance, professional bodies, ask the experts, placements and vacation work, and lots more.

Graduate Bank Accounts and Loans
http://www.namss.org.uk/banks.grad.htm
This is a very useful resource maintained by the National Association of Managers of Student Services (NAMSS). These pages compare bank accounts, loans and overdrafts designed specifically for graduates in

Searching for information...

Register now
Register with Hobsor
Services now to find
want. Members rece
membership magazin
about companies of i
fortnightly email – all
charge.

Hobsons Stud
Services
Find out about exclus
available to Hobsons
Services members in
from STA Travel and

Careers searc
Not sure where to st

the UK. This page is updated monthly from information provided by MoneyFacts

Hobsons
http://www.hobsons.com
Hobsons is a British and US-based company with over 25 years' experience in publishing educational and recruitment guides for students making career and course decisions. They provide students, advisers, parents, carers and professionals with information on courses and careers and are a premier site for details of thousands of career and education opportunities in the UK and around the world.

New Graduate
http://www.newgraduate.com
On this site you can do a job search, taking as your starting point one of several dozen employment categories. The page will then display a large number of links to recruitment agencies and other contacts specialising in that particular area, both in the UK and wider afield.

Pathfinder
http://www.pathfinder-one.com
This is an electronic version of 'the UK's number one jobhunting and career switch monthly' magazine, containing a wealth of jobs, advice and opportunities. As well as searching through Pathfinder's own online job listings, you can now search for opportunities through the UK's many other career sites, directly from Pathfinder.

Prospects Web
http://www.prospects.csu.ac.uk
Run by the Higher Education Careers Service Unit (CSU), this unmissable site offers a huge careers file for graduates. It lists job vacancies, employers, postgraduate courses and research posts in the UK and Ireland. CSU was established in 1972 to support the work of Higher Education Careers Services throughout the UK and Eire. Working in conjunction with the Association of Graduate Careers Advisory Services (AGCAS), CSU also publishes career guides and profiles for numerous areas of work, as well as computer aided careers guidance systems and software. The online content is updated each day with the latest careers information plus employment and postgraduate vacancies. Students, graduates and employers can connect directly to an online job-matching and email recruitment news service.

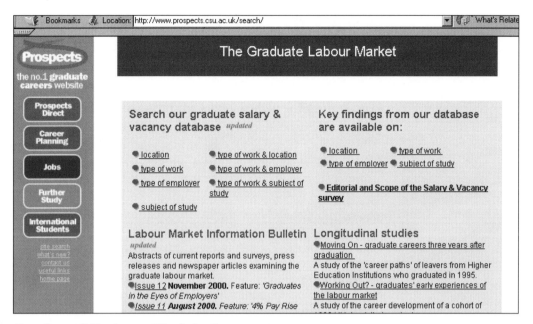

Recruitment & Employment Confederation
http://www.rec.uk.com

Fig. 10. Prospects is an authoritative source of online information about graduate employment.

The REC is the main trade organisation in the UK for recruitment firms. It has around 7,750 individual members (recruitment consultants and managers) and 6,000 corporate member offices (recruitment consultancies and employment agencies). This site is a useful resource for existing members, prospective members, graduate jobseekers, HR staff and others with an interest in recruitment issues. You can search a database of UK-based recruitment firms here.

Researcher's Guide to Job Resources
http://www.strath.ac.uk/Departments/Careers/guide/
This excellent site has been developed at the University of Strathclyde. It is aimed primarily at postgraduates and postdoctoral students looking for jobs in and out of academia. It includes both general advice sections and listings of useful internet sites arranged under various helpful categories. First comes a listing of life sciences and medical sciences sites. This is followed by an engineering/physical sciences/information technology category. The environmental sciences sites follow, and then particle physics/astronomy/maths sites. Finally comes a listing of sites for researchers working in social sciences/humanities/business/law. The site can also help you with using the internet, preparing electronic applications and CVs, using email to carry out the recruitment process, and identifying possible avenues of finding work.

Riley Guide
http://www.dbm.com/jobguide/
The established employment portal site is dedicated to employment opportunities and job resources on the internet. You can access a comprehensive and businesslike set of links covering everything from

preparing for a job search, resumes and cover letters, to targeting and researching employers, executing your job search campaign, job listings, networking, interviewing, negotiating, salary guides and guidance. There are lists of top companies, professional bodies and many useful world-wide links.

Portal sites for newspapers and magazines

▶ *Tip* – Newspapers and magazines are an important tool for graduate job hunters. They can be a valuable source of company news and economic trends, and of current job vacancies. The internet now makes it possible to explore news media all over the world from the comfort of your own desktop.

AJR NewsLink
http://www.newslink.org/news.html
The site provides lots of links to online newspapers around the world.

All Newspapers
http://www.allnewspapers.com
Offers links to top stories and to local, national, and international newspapers, magazines, electronic media, and news agencies.

Alternative Press Index
http://www.altpress.org
Founded in 1969, the API is one of the oldest self-sustaining alternative media institutions in the United States. It has been recognized as a leading guide to the alternative press in the USA and around the world. Its well-organised online directory includes publications currently indexed in its own database and members of the Independent Press Association. Subscription information, email addresses and links to home pages are included. You can browse by title and by subject.

E&P Directory of Online Newspapers
http://www.mediainfo.com/emedia/
This is a substantial database of newspapers and radio stations from all over the world. It includes a range of clearly set out search functions and listings to get you started. The database contains over 12,000 records – well worth checking out.

Ecola's Newsstand Directory
http://www.ecola.com/news/press/
Logically organized links provide easy access to periodicals worldwide. Over 8,400 newspapers and magazines are listed, all of which are maintained by a paper-printed publication, and which provide English language content online. Recommended.

Electronic Newsstand
http://www.image.dk/~knud-sor/en/
This enterprising resource contains links to a vast number and variety of international news sources, supported by quick reference regional maps. Definitely worth exploring.

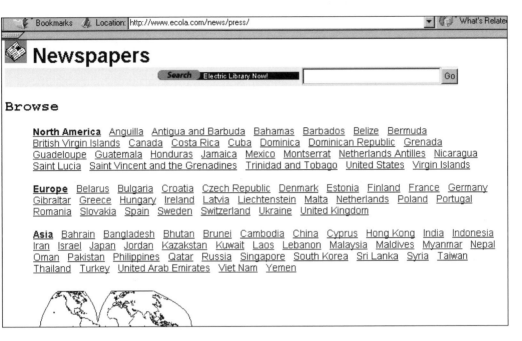

MetaGrid Newspapers & Magazines
http://www.metagrid.com/
The site enables you to search for both magazines and newspapers. Magazines are categorised by subject matter, and newspapers by continent and country.

Fig. 11. Ecola Newsstand. From here you can explore thousands of newspapers and magazines all over the world.

News Central
http://www.all-links.com/newscentral/
More than 3,500 newspaper links are currently available here.

News Directory
http://www.newsdirectory.com/
The site contains over 17,000 categorised information links.

Newslink
http://ajr.newslink.org/news.html
Here you can find listings of papers for the USA and the rest of the world.

PubList
http://www.publist.com
PubList.com is a massive internet-based reference for over 150,000 domestic and international print and electronic publications. These include magazines, journals, e-journals, newsletters, and monographs. It provides quick and easy access to detailed publication information including, titles, formats, publisher addresses, editor contacts, circulation data, and ISSN numbers. The site also provides access to subscription services as well as article-level information through rights and permissions providers and document delivery services.

Searching for information...

Other Internet Handbooks to help you

Education & Training on the Internet, Laurel Alexander.
Finding a Job on the Internet, Brendan Murphy (2nd edition).
Exploring Yahoo! on the Internet, David Holland.
Getting Started on the Internet, Kye Valongo.
Where to Find It on the Internet, Kye Valongo (2nd edition).

3 Careers services for graduates

In this chapter we will explore:

▶ *university careers services*
▶ *other online careers services*

University careers services

This section contains summaries of most of the UK university careers services which have an online presence. Descriptions are included for a few typical ones, though here is insufficient space to describe them all in detail. A more exhaustive list of such web site links – together with other institutions of higher education and complete with phone numbers and postal addresses – can be found on this useful web page:

http://www.pathfinder-one.com/Pages/Careers_Service.html

Aston
http://www.aston.ac.uk/careers/
As well as providing details of its own local services, the site contains some useful links to employers, newspapers and journals, professional bodies and careers information, overseas links, postgraduate study and research, recruitment consultancies, equal opportunity issues, and students as entrepreneurs.

Bath
http://www.bath.ac.uk/admin/careers/
Follow the link to Information for Students.

Fig. 12. The Aston University Careers Service.

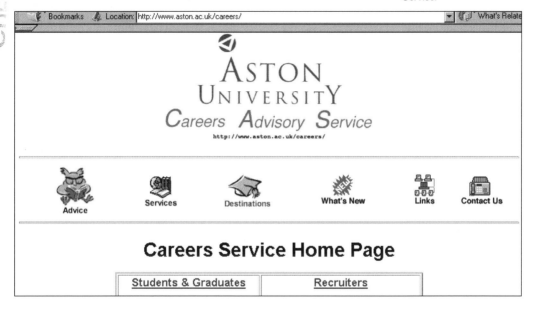

Careers services for graduates ....

Birmingham
http://www.bham.ac.uk/careers/
This excellent site includes some very useful subject specific links that have been structured to provide a research guide for careers in that subject.

Bournemouth
http://www.bournemouth.ac.uk/careers/index.html
They say: 'The Careers Service exists to provide impartial and professional advice and support to its clients. It undertakes to ensure the information and help it offers is up to date, relevant and accessible. Affiliated to the Association of Graduate Careers Advisory Services, the Careers Centre offers a range of advice, resources and services to boost your career prospects and to provide you with the career management skills necessary to make the most of your options.'

Bradford
http://www.brad.ac.uk/admin/careers/
The site includes details of graduate training schemes, internships, summer placements plus voluntary and overseas work.

Brighton
http://www.bton.ac.uk/hubs/support/careers/
The site includes a link to the Brighton Graduate Association:

http://www.bton.ac.uk/audience/former/index.htm

Bristol
http://www.cas.bris.ac.uk/
Through this site, which has the benefit of a site map, you can talk with a careers advisor, call into the information room, meet the managers, try a computerised careers program, sign up for a CareerStart course, see what jobs are around, or experience an Insight Course.

Brunel
http://http1.brunel.ac.uk:8080/admin/careers/home.shtml
Features of the site include links to employer web sites, and an interactive guide to researching employers. There are Job Hunting Resources designed to help you prepare for interviews with handouts on completing application forms, CV writing, taking aptitude tests and more. The handouts can be downloaded from here.

Cambridge
http://www.cam.ac.uk/CambUniv/Societies/cuis/
The Cambridge University Industrial Society (CUIS) is one of the largest student industrial organisations in the UK. It offers an excellent range of events that include presentations from and visits to major companies such as Ernst and Young, Arthur Andersen, and Morgan Stanley. The site has an ever-expanding list of career links, and links to the web

Site Menu

Start here
Haven't a clue?
What's on?
Job search
Vacation opportunities
Applications & interview
Postgraduate study
Careers in...
JobShop

pages of its key-group sponsors. Parts of the site require you to log in with a user name and password.

Cardiff
http://www.cf.ac.uk/uwcc/caas/index.html

Central Lancashire
http://www.uclan.ac.uk/other/student/advisory/acadadv/carer-hom.htm

City
http://www.city.ac.uk/careers/careers.html

Coventry
http://www.coventry.ac.uk/publicat/fulltime/director/careers.htm

Cranfield
http://www.cranfield.ac.uk/admin/careers/
The site benefits from a well-organised collection of graduate recruitment links, many of which are sorted by industry or country.

De Montfort
http://www.mk.dmu.ac.uk/depts/stuserv/careers/careers.html-ssi

Derby
http://www.derby.ac.uk/careers/career.html

Dublin
http://www2.tcd.ie:80/Careers/

Dundee
http://www.dundee.ac.uk/careers/

Durham
http://www.dur.ac.uk/CareersAdvice/
You can choose from undergraduate, postgraduate, graduate or employer site areas for specific focused information.

East Anglia
http://www.uea.ac.uk/ccen/
The site invites you to rate its quality by using a feedback form. In addition to the usual kind of careers advice, you will also find specific help on self-employment and entrepreneurship.

Edinburgh
http://www.careers.ed.ac.uk
The services on offer include a guide to current vacancies (Edinburgh campus only), forthcoming events, careers information, useful links, careers service staff, and an online careers service guide.

Careers
Advisory
Service

Careers services for graduates ....

Essex
http://www2.essex.ac.uk/careers
The site offers details of careers service help and events, current vacancies, vacation work opportunities and more.

Glamorgan
http://www.itc.glam.ac.uk/student/car-hom.htm

Glasgow
http://www.gla.ac.uk/Otherdepts/Careers/
This site includes careers services, links, vacation and part-time work, industrial placements, overseas opportunities, postgraduate study and funding and graduates recruiters.

Fig. 13. The Glasgow University Careers Service.

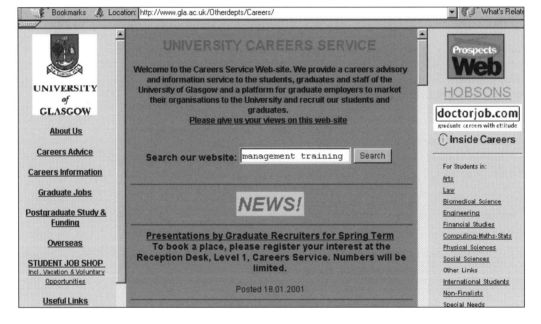

Heriot-Watt
http://www.hw.ac.uk/careers/
The Careers Advisory Service offers advice and information to first, second and third year students, final year and postgraduate students and graduates, to help them plan and implement their career choice. This includes: one-to-one careers advice, assisted guidance, information and seminars on self employment, voluntary work, CVs and interview techniques, aptitude tests, job options, further study, graduate employers, plus graduate, part-time, and vacation job vacancy details.

Huddersfield
http://www.hud.ac.uk/careers/
Registration is required for access to parts of this service.

Hull
http://www.hull.ac.uk/careers
The service makes information available to students, graduates, employers and future students about recruitment and study opportunities in the UK and overseas.

Imperial College London
http://www.ad.ic.ac.uk/registry/careers/
The site includes vacancy listings, vacation work opportunities, links to employers, jobs and careers related sites, and information for people with disabilities.

Keele
http://www.keele.ac.uk/depts/aa/Careers/home.htm

Kent
http://www.ukc.ac.uk/careers/

Kings College London Career Services
http://www.kcl.ac.uk/kis/college/careers/links/links.htm
This is a large site hosted by Kings College London Career Services on behalf of the University of London Careers Service. There are links to career choice, further study, job hunting resources, regional and international working, self employment, voluntary and vacation work and employer web sites.

Kingston
http://www.kingston.ac.uk/users/cc_s416/cas/cashome.htm

Lancaster
http://www.comp.lancs.ac.uk/uni-services/careers/careers.html

Leeds
http://www.leeds.ac.uk/careers/
The online careers centre includes a special graduates' section. This includes a general listing of UK recruitment agencies.

Leeds Metropolitan
http://www.lmu.ac.uk/aqd/careers/

Leicester
http://www.le.ac.uk/careers/

Lincolnshire and the Humber
http://www.humber.ac.uk

Liverpool
http://www.liv.ac.uk/ccap/index.htm
The site includes a feature called *Next Move*, which contains news, vacancies and information for final-year students, postgraduates and

recent graduates. You can either view them online, or download them as PDF files which you can view at leisure using Acrobat Reader.

Liverpool John Moores
http://cwis.livjm.ac.uk/careers/

London
http://www.careers.lon.ac.uk/
As you would expect for a higher education institution of this size, this is a massive site with literally thousands of well-organised links covering every aspect of careers guidance, job search and vacancies. To take just a single example, there are links to more than 600 professional and trade associations, institutions and societies which often have useful information on their particular career area or relevant news.

Loughborough
http://info.lut.ac.uk/service/careers/index.html

Luton
http://www.luton.ac.uk/careers/services/careersadvice.html

Manchester and UMIST
http://www.netwise.ac.uk/
The Manchester and UMIST Careers Service operates online as Netwise. In addition to general careers information and links, including a Recruitment Mall, there is help for various special interest groups including international students, mature students, students with disabilities and ethnic minority students.

Fig. 14. The Manchester University/UMIST Careers Service, Netwise.

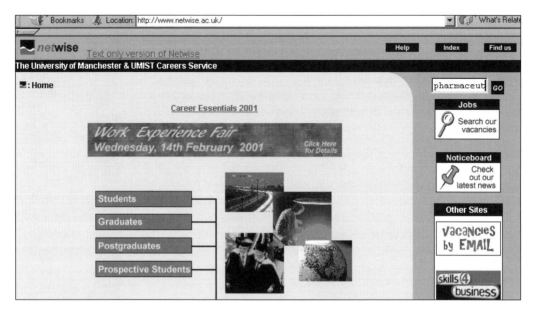

Manchester Metropolitan
http://cra.als.aca.mmu.ac.uk/careers/careers.htm

Middlesex
http://www.mdx.ac.uk/www/careers/

Napier
http://www.napier.ac.uk/depts/careers/cashome.html

Newcastle
http://www.careers.ncl.ac.uk

Nottingham
http://www.nottingham.ac.uk/careers/

Northumbria
http://www.unn.ac.uk/academic/hswe/careers/index2.html
This is a huge site put together by the University of Northumbria's Careers Guidance and Counselling department. You can link into training and employment as a career advisor and over 1,500 active links to relevant sites. The links cover the full range of relevant academic disciplines – plus education, training and employment links – and economic, political and social information relevant to the work of the career adviser. There is a smaller list of links to those UK and EU organisations that have information on career opportunities.

Nottingham Trent
http://www.ntu.ac.uk/acs/careers/index.html

Oxford
http://www.careers.ox.ac.uk/
Oxford University Careers Service (OUCS) provides information to students, graduates, employers, and future students about recruitment and further study in the UK. There is also a guide to vacation work, and how to user the internet effectively. There are links to the MBA Careers Service, employers, commercial intermediaries, newspapers and journals, study, associations, international careers information, and miscellaneous other resources.

Oxford Brookes
http://www.brookes.ac.uk/student/services/careers/

Plymouth
http://www.plymouth.ac.uk/services/careers/careers.htm

Portsmouth
http://www.port.ac.uk/student.services/careers/

Queen's University of Belfast
http://www.qub.ac.uk/co/

Careers services for graduates ....

Careers Ser
Home Pages | University
Useful links | Back |

Student Employm

- Opening Hours
- Code of Practice
- Students
- University Staff
- Employers
- Students @ Work

Reading
http://www.rdg.ac.uk/Careers/

Royal Holloway
http://vms.rhbnc.ac.uk/ ~ uhye032/careers.html

Salford
http://www.salford.ac.uk/careers/
The careers advisory page at Salford University has links to: where are we, stop press, what's on, jobs, placements and vacation work, a job shop, careers advisers, getting started, careers doctor, postgraduates, students with disabilities, information for employers, and miscellaneous links. The links section is substantial and broad in scope, and is based on the AGCAS occupational index system.

Sheffield
http://www.shef.ac.uk/uni/services/cas/

Sheffield Hallam
http://www.shu.ac.uk/services/ssc/careers/

South Bank
http://www.sbu.ac.uk/careers/

Southampton
http://www.soton.ac.uk/ ~ careers/

Staffordshire
http://www.staffs.ac.uk/sands/care/CareersService.html

Stirling
http://www.stir.ac.uk/theuni/suinfo/careers/

Strathclyde
http://www.strath.ac.uk/Departments/Careers/
They say: 'We deal with over 40,000 enquiries each year from students, graduates, University administrators, academic colleagues, employers and government departments and agencies so we already know what many of you are thinking! This web site will provide you with much of the information you may be seeking.'

Sunderland
http://www.sunderland.ac.uk/student-careers-service/index.htm

Sussex
http://www.susx.ac.uk/Units/CDU/
The Sussex University Career Development Unit is intended for current students and graduates from the University of Sussex. Features of the service include an information centre, talking to a careers adviser, special interest groups (students with disabilities, ethnic minority students and

---

2000 graduates!
form? We'd love to
on the survey, em

Vacancies Today

If you are looking
the Where do I st

Use the links on th

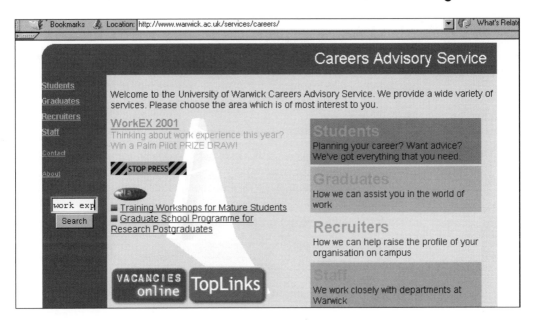

Fig. 15. The Warwick University Careers Service.

lesbian and gay students), postgraduate study, workshops, employer presentations and briefings, publications, vacancy information, and the Sussex Graduate Network.

Wales (Aberystwyth)
http://www.aber.ac.uk/ ~ carwww/careers.html

Wales (Bangor)
http://www.bangor.ac.uk/careers/

Wales (Swansea)
http://www.swan.ac.uk/careers

Warwick
http://www.warwick.ac.uk/services/careers/

West of England
http://www.uwe.ac.uk/careers/
This is a substantial careers information site, and one that benefits from a comprehensive site map and alphabetical index.

Westminster
http://www.wmin.ac.uk/StudServ/Careers/careers.html

Wolverhampton
http://www.wlv.ac.uk/careers/main/index.htm
The web site includes details of the careers guidance and information service, the part time employment bureau (USEB), and the West Midlands Mentoring Scheme for ethnic minority students.

Careers services for graduates ....

York

http://www.york.ac.uk/services/careers/

If you like to see what happened to some recent students, it is interesting to follow the link to Destinations of York Graduates. After graduation, most history students for example appear to have followed careers in management, administration and finance.

Other online careers services

All kinds of careers services are available online today. Most are free to users, the costs of maintaining the web sites being covered by advertising or sponsorship. A few do make charges for CV services and individual advice facilities. Many are American, but an increasing number of UK and other local sites can be found. You can get help with such topics as:

1. writing CVs and covering letters
2. interview technique
3. jobsearch
4. career planning and development

1st Impact

http://www.1st-imp.com

This is a site offers resume writing, employment, and career management resources. Follow the links to jobsearch, career café, career news, the gold mine, reading room, career counsellor and bookstore.

A Better Career

http://www.abc.vg

Here you can find some hard hitting and in-depth articles written for everyone interested in advancing their career by the effective use of CVs.

Activate

http://www.activatecareers.co.uk

This is a leading interactive multimedia graduate recruitment directory. Site features include a graduate career search and CV builder. They say: 'Use our comprehensive search engine to pinpoint the company of your choice, where they are based, who they're looking for, what they pay and the long term prospects they hope to offer. All graduate career entries are cross-linked and companies are grouped by industry sector and profession to enable you to focus your career research. In summary you have the most up-to-date graduate recruitment resource at your fingertips to help you in your quest for a great future.'

Adset

http://www.adset-plus.co.uk

This site is concerned with providing information about learning opportunities, and offers details of its own publications, training, research and consultancy services.

Alec's Free CV, Job Hunting & Interview Tips
http://www.alec.co.uk
This site offers practical commonsense advice for jobseekers. The services range from tips on getting a foot in the door to careers guidance. There is also the offer of a professional CV writing service.

BBC Knowledge: Work it Up
http://www.bbc.co.uk/knowledge/home/index.shtml
This site links in with the BBC digital television programme to provide essential careers information. It features a different sector of work each week.

Bradley CVs
http://www.bradleycvs.co.uk
You can pay a fee to have a professionally written CV, and get advice on seeking and securing jobs on this site. There are also plenty of links to recruitment sites.

Buzzword Career Management
http://www.buzzwordcv.com
This company offers a broad range of services to assist managing and developing careers. It contains links to a number of sister sites offering careers-related information and databases.

CareerBuilder
http://www.careerbuilder.com
This site provides advice on résumé writing (including electronic ones), links to career information, features and career management tools.

Fig. 16. Career Builder.

Careers services for graduates ....

CareerLab
http://www.careerlab.com
This is the site of a career and human resources consulting firm. Its product line includes career counselling, management testing and assessment, executive coaching, performance improvement, 360-degree reviews, teambuilding, and outplacement. A feature of the site is its collection of readymade covering letters.

CareerMatch
http://www.intec.edu.za/career/career.htm
CareerMatch offers a quick way to get free, personal vocational guidance. All you do is fill out a form that involves the ranking of various describing words. You submit your form online and within seconds you should receive your personal CareerMatch results. When you submit your questionnaire to Intec for evaluation, its programme is able to determine a unique profile in terms of six of your most significant characteristics or personality attributes. Using this profile, it compares and matches it against similar profiles established for about 100 different careers.

Career Help

How to Be Wanted

Outstanding CV's

Personal Marketing

Interview Skills

Career Management

CareerSign
http://www.careersign.com
CareerSign is a London-based source of research-based advice, guidance and information to help individuals to improve their career management skills. It includes a Career Talk UK Community, help with graduate CVs and many other features.

Career Solutions
http://www.careersolutions.co.uk
You will find this a user-friendly, detailed site including advice about CVs and interviews, and job listings links.

Careers Research and Advisory Centre
http://www.crac.org.uk
Established for 35 years, CRAC is an independent agency that supports lifelong learning and career development. It provides authoritative training material and careers information for young people looking to make those all-important choices for the future. CRAC draws together key organisations from industry, academic institutions, consultants and professional bodies to create a network of career development opportunities.

CareerWorld
http://www.careerworld.net
This site offers a free service to people about to leave school, college or university in the UK. It provides detailed career advice, job vacancies, vocational guidance and gap year choices together with university and college opportunities at both further and higher education.

CareerZone UK

http://www.careerzone-uk.com

This site offers impartial advice and information on all aspects of career, employment, education and training advice in the UK. Visit the online library, bookshop and careers clinic. You can also access over 5,000 vacancies.

CV Special

http://www.cvspecial.co.uk

CV Special is a site well worth visiting. It oozes expertise and professionalism and offers users a great deal of free and very useful hints and guidelines on getting their CV and covering letters right. They say: 'This CV service has helped over 3,000 clients in 10 years, at all levels in every occupation you could think of and all parts of the world.'

Doctor Job (GTI Careerscape)

http://www.doctorjob.co.uk

This dynamic site from Oxfordshire-based publishing company GTI contains details of vacancies, careers advice and information about top employers for graduates in the UK. It also features advice about opportunities for postgraduates. If you're stuck for answers and need some professional advice, it has an expert online every month who can help solve your more troubling careers problems.

Graduate Base

http://www.graduatebase.com

Graduate Base offers advice, career planning, and recruitment for UK students and graduates. It uses down-to-earth and accessible language to match the right companies with the right graduates. It allows gradu-

Fig. 17. Graduate Base.

57

ates to choose the career that suits their strengths from getting a foot in the door, to making the most of an interview opportunity and dealing with job offers.

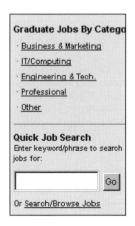

Graduate Link

http://www.graduatelink.com

Graduate Link operates on behalf of thirteen university and higher education colleges in Yorkshire and Humberside to promote graduate recruitment in local companies. It offers advice and graduate recruitment services to employers, and helps graduates find employment in the region all year round. It is supported by the European Social Fund.

Inside Careers

http://www.insidecareers.co.uk

This site offers a guide to ten leading UK professions plus career advice, details of key recruiters and postgraduate courses and job vacancies. It covers actuaries, accountants, engineering, information technology, logistics management, attorneys, management consultants, and tax advisers. You can apply to be kept informed by email of last-minute vacancies, recruitment drives, and site developments.

JobBank USA

http://www.jobbankusa.com

JobBank USA specialises in providing career information including job and resume database services to job candidates, employers and recruitment firms in the US and worldwide.

Job Interview Network

http://www.job-interview.net

This is a fascinating site featuring job interview tips, questions and answers (related to over 40 professions and job functions) plus sample interview questions.

Kaleidoscopic

http://www.kaleidoscopic.co.uk

This is an attractively produced printed and online magazine designed primarily for black and Asian students and graduates. It offers a variety of features and editorial content, including a discussion forum, plus a list of some graduate recruiters and links to their pages.

Milkround Online

http://www.milkround.co.uk

Founded in 1997 and based in Soho, London, this specialist service links 'top undergraduates' with the companies who want to employ them in such fields as management consultancy, advertising, and City of London financial services. Milkround has created a dominant brand within its target market place. Its management combines a wide range of experience ranging from consulting and investment banking through to IT and civil engineering. Its core team is supported by a network of freelancers. The team members are all graduates themselves.

Monster Board UK
http://www.monster.co.uk
This version is the UK offspring of the original US Monster Board and offers a variety of careers advisory and support services.

National Business Employment Weekly
http://careers.wsj.com
This is a US-based career guidance and job search publication. Subscribers are promised the latest on business and franchising opportunities. The site includes an index for job hunters outside the USA as well as feature articles, archive and special discount info.

Professional CVs and Résumés
http://www.edinburghconcepts.com/cv_homepage.htm
This site offers free CV and résumé tips plus interview resources, job links and more.

Proteus
http://www.proteus-net.co.uk
Founded in 1989, Proteus is one of the UK's largest career guidance and training organisations. It provides a total career service designed to resolve just about any career or career guidance problem. Redundancy, blocked progress, job dissatisfaction or even the wrong career are typical of the situations facing its clients. You can access help with career guidance, a database of key British enterprises, the Executive Grapevine (for executives) and more general job databases through this consultancy. It receives details of more than 500,000 jobs a year, making it one of the most complete and up-to-date resources on the internet.

Red Mole
http://www.redmole.co.uk
This is an underground magazine for students and recent graduates still searching for work. The knowledge exchange is there to help students struggling with essays and the like ... or those who are simply lazy. You will find lots of useful advice here.

Skills for Work
http://www.man.ac.uk/careers/SkillsForWork/
This site details a report by the University of Manchester and the UMIST Careers Service which examines the skills developed by higher education and how they relate to skills required by graduate employers.

Topcareers
http://www.topcareers.net
The site features a top graduate career guide, top technical graduate guide, and an MBA career guide.

RESUME DATABASE

Register your credentials with the Web's most confidential resume database.
↳ **GO**

JOB AGENT

Create a JobSeek Agent and receive new job listings by e-mail that match your criteria.
↳ **GO**

Careers services for graduates ....

Fig. 18. Red Mole Jobs.

World Careers Network
http://www.wcn.co.uk/main/
This is a guide on how to get on for graduates. Register for access to job vacancy listings, worldwide companies database, employment search and career fairs information.

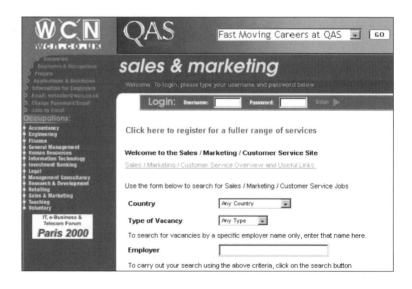

More Internet Handbooks to help you

Careers Guidance on the Internet, Laurel Alexander.
Finding a Job on the Internet, Brendan Murphy (2nd edition).

4 Gaining additional qualifications

In this chapter we will explore:

▶ *distance and online courses*
▶ *vocational and skills training*
▶ *postgraduate study*
▶ *research councils and other funding bodies*

· ·

Once you have completed your first degree, you may want to enhance your employability profile by arming yourself with some additional quali-fications. This chapter introduces some of the best-known distance and online study and training services, plus opportunities for postgraduate qualifications, research and support.

Distance and online courses

Continuing and Distance Education Links
http://www.cde.psu.edu/users/atb/main.htm
This site contains links to internet resources in the fields of continuing and distance education. From the home page you can link to computer support, distance education, instructional design resources, student resources and www information and much more.

Distance Learning
http://www.distance-learning.co.uk
In association with the Open University, the Distance Learning web site contains details of international distance and open education and training worldwide. You can explore course providers, accountancy, finance and economics, applied science, arts and humanities, building and planning, business and administration, communications, computer science and information technology, education and training, examinations, law, leisure, management, medicine, pure science and maths, and social sciences.

Distance Learning Centre
http://www.user.globalnet.co.uk/ ~ dlc/index.htm
If you would like a British qualification which will help you gain entry into nurse training or initial teacher training, the DLC can offer you a kite-marked access course validated by the Open College Network. You can work at home but maintain a direct link to your own personal tutor through the internet, by post or by telephone.

Distance Learning on the Net
http://www.hoyle.com/distance.htm
This is a useful page of links for online and distance learning. Included are descriptions of distance education web sites, along with links to lead you to further distance learning and education resources on the net.

Gaining additional qualifications ....

Get Educated

http://www.geteducated.com

Get Educated publishes a free directory of online colleges, internet universities and training institutes, so you can take a quick trip around the growing number of virtual campuses on the information superhighway. If you can't find what you are looking, check the 'free articles for distance learners' section of the resource centre. If you want a comprehensive guide to accredited virtual graduate schools, you can consult its guide to the virtual university movement, *Best Distance Learning Graduate Schools: Earning Your Degree Without Leaving Home*, published by the Princeton Review and Random House. This guide profiles 195 graduate programmes in the United States and abroad.

Globewide Network Academy

http://www.gnacademy.org

GNA is an educational non-profit organisation established to assist in all aspects of virtual and distance learning. Its Online Distance Education Catalogue lists a staggering 17,000 courses and programs. It also consults on the development of virtual organisations and training materials. You can visit the online student or teacher lounge, bookstore, links to academic support, or contact them.

International Centre for Distance Learning

http://www-icdl.open.ac.uk

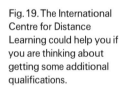

Fig. 19. The International Centre for Distance Learning could help you if you are thinking about getting some additional qualifications.

This is a site originated by the Open University and the ICDL. It is an international centre for research, teaching, consultancy, information and publishing activities. From the home page you can access databases on literature, institutions and courses. You can find out how to get a qualification in open and distance education. One icon on the home page will take you to ICDL services, another will take you to the bulletin board, and another to collaborative projects.

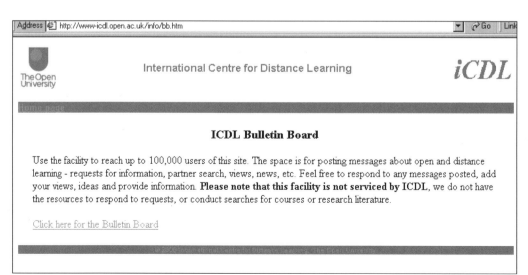

Address | http://www-icdl.open.ac.uk/info/bb.htm | ▼ | ⟳ Go | Link

The Open University   International Centre for Distance Learning   *iCDL*

Home page

ICDL Bulletin Board

Use the facility to reach up to 100,000 users of this site. The space is for posting messages about open and distance learning - requests for information, partner search, views, news, etc. Feel free to respond to any messages posted, add your views, ideas and provide information. **Please note that this facility is not serviced by ICDL, we do not have the resources to respond to requests, or conduct searches for courses or research literature.**

Click here for the Bulletin Board

International Correspondence Schools
http://www.icslearn.com/
ICS is the largest distance learning training organisation in the world. During the last few years it has been expanding its services to include home, business, and industry subjects.

International School of Information Management
http://www.isimu.edu/
ISIM is an accredited provider of distance education and training. It offers graduate degrees in business administration and information management. In addition to graduate degree programs, ISIM offers corporate training programs, and classes for continuing education in a number of career-enhancing courses for the adult professional.

Learning over the Internet
http://www.unc.edu/cit/guides/irg-38.html
From this page you can link to colleges, universities, and other educational institutions that are teaching classes or delivering course materials over the internet. There are links to directories of online courses, syllabuses, course materials, and examples of online classes. Also included are links to consortia and other organisations devoted to delivering distance education with networked technologies.

LifeLong Learning
http://www.lifelonglearning.com
This site offers a database of distance learning courses, scholarships for online degrees, information on financing your lifelong learning, and a specific section on adult learning resources.

McGraw-Hill Lifetime Learning
http://www.mhlifetimelearning.com/
McGraw-Hill is one of the world's biggest publishers of educational, management and science books and materials. Its web site offers internet and offline correspondence courses, print-based materials, computer-based training and multimedia plus courses for private individuals and organisations.

National Extension College
http://www.nec.ac.uk
The NEC specialises in supported home study courses and learning resources for professionals. The home page has a multitude of links. The green area is split into three sections: one with several links related to NEC (e.g. contacts and equal opportunities), the second with links related to its learning programme divisions (e.g. courses and student information and the third column links you into the learning resources division (e.g. tutor/training resources).

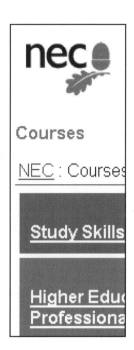

National Grid for Learning
http://www.ngfl.gov.uk/ngfl/index.html
The NGFL is the UK government's official hub for learning on the internet. From the home page you can link to schools, further education, higher

education, lifelong learning, career development, libraries, links, government and agencies and learning resources. Other hyperlinks will take you to search, advice, feedback and discussion groups.

National Open College Network
http://www.nocn.ac.uk
The NOCN offers a comprehensive accreditation service through a national framework of local Open College Networks. You can link into the NOCN Qualifications Directory, open college networks, news, events, unit library, members' information and NOCN qualifications.

Online Learning
http://www.onlinelearning.net/
Online Learning is an online supplier of continuing higher education, dedicated to providing busy professionals with the tools needed to pursue their lifelong learning objectives. You can choose from a menu of certificated and sequential online programs and courses designed with your career in mind.

Open University
http://www.open.ac.uk
The OU is Britain's largest and most innovative university. Founded by Royal Charter in 1969, it has grown rapidly both in student numbers and in its range of courses. There are professional development programmes in management, education, health and social welfare, manufacturing and computer applications, as well as self-contained study packs.

Vocational and skills training

4Training.com
http://www.4training.com
This site offers links to all kinds of training opportunities such as computer training, safety training, corporate training, vocational training, information and resources. There are also links to related sites e.g. 4Universities and 4Colleges.

American Society for Training and Development
http://www.astd.org
This is a site for workplace learning and development. You can access links to the marketplace (jobs, conferences and books), a library facility and ASTD's communities of practice (different subject areas), products and services, forums, research and policies.

Business Information Zone
http://www.thebiz.co.uk
This site is a UK business directory which incorporates a virtual training zone. This links you to a virtual training calendar (training courses) and a virtual training library (products). A search function takes you into pages of further links related to your chosen area. For each title you will find pricing details, a short description of the product or service and an enquiry form for further information.

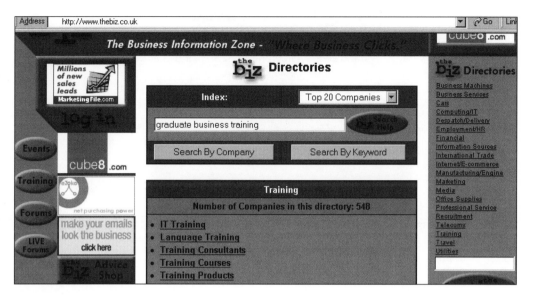

Telelink Training for Europe
http://www.marble.ac.uk/telep/telework/tlpfolder/tlp.html
The TeleLink Training for Europe project is a European Community, Euroform-funded project which seeks to develop training opportunities in the field of teleworking.

Fig. 20. Business Information Zone ('The Biz') is an established online directory of UK commercial firms and other organisations.

Training and Enterprise Councils
http://www.tec.co.uk
This site links into geographical index, news, a links page and discussion forum.

Training Pages
http://www.trainingpages.co.uk
Training Pages is a source of information for professional training products and services, and a directory of professional business management and IT training courses in the UK. You can search by listing or keyword.

Training Zone
http://www.trainingzone.co.uk
You can visit this site to check out the latest news, resources, and directories. You can access online events, products and human resources. There are various links, a search facility, latest postings and discussion forums.

Training Resources
http://www.geocities.com/Athens/Acropolis/3982/training.html
This site offers links to a number of training and development sites including UK Training Pages, Centre for Workforce Development and ASTD Training Marketplace among others.

Gaining additional qualifications ································

Training SuperSite
http://www.trainingsupersite.com
You can visit resources, publications, software download, job bank, the learning centre, directories, research and chatrooms.

Postgraduate opportunities

Edition XII
http://www.editionxii.co.uk
The organisation publishes an MBA directory and information on distance learning.

Financial Aid for study in the USA
http://www.finaid.org

Fulbright Commission
http://www.fulbright.co.uk
The Fulbright Commission is a key source of for information on courses and funding in the United States.

Hobsons MBA
http://www.mba.hobsons.com
This site will help you choose a suitable MBA course.

Hobsons Postgraduate
http://www.postgrad.hobsons.com
You can do a database search here for postgraduate courses and research opportunities.

Fig. 21. This excellent guide to MBA and postgraduate courses is maintained by the National Association of Managers of Student Services (NAMSS).

MBA and Postgraduate Courses
http://www.namss.org.uk/mba.htm
This excellent resource is maintained by the National Association of Managers of Student Services (NAMSS). It covers MBA and postgraduate information, courses, research degrees and application resources.

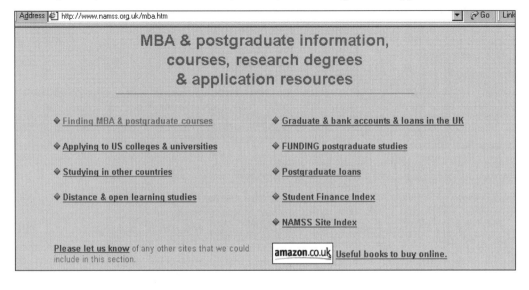

Address http://www.namss.org.uk/mba.htm ▼ 𝒫 Go Link

MBA & postgraduate information, courses, research degrees & application resources

◆ Finding MBA & postgraduate courses   ◆ Graduate & bank accounts & loans in the UK

◆ Applying to US colleges & universities   ◆ FUNDING postgraduate studies

◆ Studying in other countries   ◆ Postgraduate loans

◆ Distance & open learning studies   ◆ Student Finance Index

                                                ◆ NAMSS Site Index

Please let us know of any other sites that we could include in this section.   amazon.co.uk Useful books to buy online.

Merlin Falcon
http://www.merlinfalcon.co.uk
The site contains a useful database of postgraduate opportunities.

NISS Postgraduate and Postdoctoral Noticeboard
http://www.niss.ac.uk/cr/careers/postgrad.html
NISS is an established UK academic portal site maintained by some of the leading institutions in higher education.

PhD Jobs
http://www.phdjobs.com
This is an online job search and career advice service for postgraduates, run by the ECI Postgraduate Careers Service. It features a database of vacancies in industry and academia, details of forthcoming seminars and information for recruiters.

Fig. 22. PhD Jobs is an essential bookmark for postgraduate job hunters.

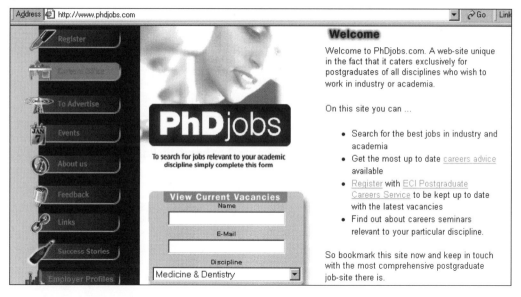

Postgraduates International Network
http://www.postgrad.org/

Prospects for Postgraduates
http://www.prospects.csu.ac.uk
The site maintains a database of opportunities for postgraduates.

Teacher Training Agency
http://www.teach.org.uk
Here you can search for PGCE courses with vacancies.

Teaching Company Directorate
http://www.tcd.co.uk
This site offers access to a number of schemes which combine postgraduate study and jobs in industry.

Gaining additional qualifications ....

Program Menu _ Resource Menu __ Text Menu --What's New

What Is The Applicant Support Network?

The Applicant Support Network helps you craft the most effective application possible for graduate and undergraduate schools. The network, which is sponsored by Career Advisor Associates, shows you how admissions committees view your application as a single unified story, not as a set of discrete components such as board scores and grades. On this network, we present information and access to resources that will help you write the most effective application possible.

The founders of Career Advisor Associates, who themselves have reviewed actual admissions files for leading graduate programs, understand how to help you prepare a unified application. We created the free Applicant Support Network to provide inside information about the workings of the selection process and describe those steps which you must complet to develop an effective application. We have also gathered information about the multitude of resources , both on and off-line, which can help you with specific portions of the process.

How To Use The Network

Research councils and other funding bodies

Applicant Support Network
http://wl.iglou.com/asn/
The organisation can help with applications for postgraduate study in USA.

Arts and Humanities Research Board
http://www.ahrb.ac.uk

Association of Medical Research Charities
http://www.amrc.org.uk
The Association can offer help for those wishing to apply for grants from member organisations.

Biotechnology and Biological Sciences Research Council
http://www.bbsrc.ac.uk

5 Current vacancies

In this chapter we will explore:

▶ *graduate recruitment agencies*
▶ *online jobs and CV databases*

. . . .

Graduate recruitment agencies

A1 Assured Recruitment
http://www.a1assured.com
This is a specialist IT recruitment agency, covering contract and permanent jobs throughout the UK. You can submit your CV online, and take advantage of its referral scheme.

Accounting Web
http://www.accountingweb.co.uk
This site offers lists of accountancy firm, links, databases, discussion, library and search. The job section contains links to a collection of online recruitment sites to which you are invited to subscribe. There is access to over a million live company reports from Companies House.

ActiJob (Canada)
http://www.actijob.com
From the home page of this site you can access hundreds of job opportunities in English or French. There are links to the job-chat centre and further employment and recruitment sites.

Acumen
http://www.acumenonline.com
Acumen is a contract and permanent personnel agency which provides staffing services to the pharmaceutical, biotech and healthcare industries throughout the UK. It provides personnel for engineering, technical, scientific and manufacturing environments. The site is directed mainly at client organisations. A useful feature of the site is its links to leading UK and international chemicals and pharmaceutical employers.

jobs

Engineering

Agency Central
http://www.agencycentral.co.uk
Agency Central enables candidates to search for an IT agency by name, county and skill set. CVs can also be submitted online for subscribed agencies to view at their leisure.

Alba International
http://www.alba.net
Alba is a recruitment and contracting company to the major oil and gas companies throughout the world from its head office in the Isle of Man, with offices in Azerbaijan, Kuwait and Malaysia. You can visit these pages to explore opportunities in oil and gas recruitment worldwide.

Current vacancies ....

Alba has a computerised database of over 8,000 fully qualified and experienced oil and gas personnel to cover the requirements of the industry.

Angel International Recruitment
http://www.angel-int.co.uk
Angel promotes the placing of temporary staff within the commercial, medical, hotel catering and driving arenas. This site has a very straightforward feedback form that can be used to declare an interest in a particular service.

Appointments for Teachers
http://www.aft.co.uk
This site presently displays over 1,550 primary and secondary school jobs. You can also click onto teacher supply agencies and overseas teaching.

Fig. 23. Appointments for Teachers.

Astbury Marsden
http://astburymarsden.co.uk
Astbury Marsden is an established name in IT and financial recruitment. The company offers opportunities in six divisions: information technology, middle office banking, commerce and industry, corporate finance, equity research and international sectors. Each section is derived into current vacancies listed by job type and each job is explained in full.

Austin Knight
http://www.austinknight.com
Austin Knight is a long-established player in the recruitment world. The company was founded in 1921 and has offices worldwide. This site features 'cybercruiting' whereby job adverts are viewed by those who need to see them but might not normally visit third party recruitment companies.

Badenoch & Clark
http://www.badenochandclark.com
Badenoch & Clark was established in 1980 as a specialist financial recruitment consultancy. It expanded into the legal and banking markets and then in the mid-1990s into the public sector and IT contracting markets. Today it has 12 offices with over 300 consultants and around 80 support staff.

Balfour Associates
http://www.balfour.co.uk
Balfour is a London-based information technology recruitment agency. There is online candidate registration, and searchable database of vacancies. Alternatively, you can browse for vacancies in engineering and IT.

Beament Leslie Thomas
http://www.blt.co.uk
BLT provides a specialist recruitment service concerned with tax, management consultancy and public finance. Check out Careerwatch, a service that enables those not necessarily desperate for a change to keep up to date with opportunities. CVs are held and sent to companies only with job-seeker permission – useful if you are still in employment and you don't particularly want referees to be contacted.

* HR Generalists
* Recruitment & Sel
* Compensation & B
* Training & Develo
* HR Strategy & Pol
* Change Managem
* Employment Law

Beechwood Recruitment
http://www.appointmentsregister.co.uk
Beechwood is a London-based engineering, IT and science recruitment agency, with some graduate positions.

Bluestone
http://www.bluestone.ltd.uk
Based in the City of London, Bluestone specialises in financial services recruitment. It attracts clients from a whole range of organisations from investment banks to insurance providers as well as the leading professional service suppliers. It recruits across a wide spectrum of skills for roles within consulting, managerial and technical job functions. It focuses on selective search and advertising. Its databases hold details of experienced individuals discreetly seeking new career opportunities.

Brackman Kinsey Durrant
http://www.brackman-kinsey.com
This London agency offers permanent and contract positions in banking, finance and computing, throughout the UK.

Bryon Employment (Australia)
http://www.bryon.com.au
This site operates mainly as a job-listing service and offers a massive selection of jobs around Australia. There are also links to Australian employment-related resources.

Current vacancies ....

Capital Recruitment
http://www.cap-recruit.co.uk
Capital Recruitment is a London-based recruitment agency serving the aviation, telecommunications, electrical, and engineering fields.

Capstan Teachers
http://www.capstan.co.uk/
If you are a teacher, whether UK or overseas trained, UK-based Capstan offers access to primary and secondary short and long-term posts. The site includes an introduction, guidance for students and newly qualified teachers, brief information about working in or coming from the European Union, Australia, New Zealand, United States, Canada and elsewhere.

Careers in Construction
http://www.careersinconstruction.com
From the home page of this site, you can access jobs (architecture, consultants, contractors, surveyors), CV service, offshore jobs, training and resources for freelancers.

Charity People
http://www.charitypeople.co.uk
This is the site of a recruitment consultancy specialising in the not-for-profit sector. You can link into vacancies and charitable and government bodies.

Christopher Keats Media Recruitment
http://www.christopherkeats.co.uk
Established in 1987, the company places staff in jobs in broadcasting, advertising, publishing, public relations, marketing and design. Brief details are given of the vacancies, which are mainly secretarial and administrative, and salaries. The site includes lists of clients in each category, with hyperlinks to the home pages of some of them.

City Executive Consultants
http://www.cityexec.co.uk
CEC recruits for the financial services sector in the City of London, providing candidates for investment banking, securities and fund management. The site presents detailed information about current vacancies, and supplies a comprehensive CV-style response form for applicants to use online.

Civil Service Jobs
http://www.open.gov.uk/co/fsaesd/ukjobs.htm
The Civil Service is among the largest graduate recruiters in the country. Graduates enter mainly through departmental and agency recruitment schemes, although small numbers are also recruited through the fast stream entry schemes. This comprehensive but dull web site contains an enormous list of all the categories of civil servants they wish to recruit.

Computer People Online
http://www.computerpeople.co.uk
Visit a first class online job finder (permanent and contract) from the long-established IT recruitment company with offices all over the UK and Ireland. This site offers a good way for computer professionals to seek out that next step up the career ladder.

CPL Scientific Employment Services
http://www.cplscientific.co.uk/ses/
CPL provides contingency recruitment services to companies through-out the UK. These include the supply of permanent and contract staff at all levels from technicians to managers, as well as payroll services. Its assignments are in the life science and chemical industries, including biotechnology, environment, fine chemicals, food and pharmaceuticals. The service uses a national database of more than 6,000 applicants on a no-placement no-fee basis. It is free to applicants, and has around 25 to 30 jobs open at any time. The company is based in Newbury, Berkshire.

Crone Corkill
http://www.cronecorkill.co.uk
Crone Corkill provides temporary, permanent, and part-time administra-tors, executives and linguists.

Crossley House Recruitment
http://www.chr.co.uk
Look here for executive search and selection services for the food, man-ufacturing and engineering, sales and marketing, healthcare, and finance sectors.

Douglas Llambias Associates
http://www.llambias.co.uk
London-based DLA is a leading provider of financial, IT and other spe-cialist recruitment services to accountancy and legal firms, industrial and commercial companies, management consultancies and banking and financial services organisations, both nationally and internationally. The site contained several hundred vacancies, presented under broad indus-try categories, with brief details of each, including remuneration levels and online application forms.

Earthworks
http://ourworld.compuserve.com/homepages/eworks/
You will find careers, jobs and training opportunities for all disciplines related to earth sciences including ecology, geocomputing, archaeology, oceanography, mining and astronomy plus more on this site.

ELT Job Vacancies
http://www.jobs.edunet.com
This is a good contact point for English language teaching posts any-where in the world.

Salary:	Any sala
Job Title:	Any Job
Location:	Any Loca / Amsterda / City of L / Dockland / Europe / Greater L
Language:	Include L
Keyword :	

Current vacancies ....

Euro Hotel Jobs
http://www.eurohoteljobs.com
If you are looking for a job in the hotel industry in Europe, this is the page for you.

European Resources
http://www.e-r.co.uk
This is the site of a top recruitment agency specialising in graduates and others with language skills.

Executive Recruitment Services
http://www.ers.co.uk
Opportunities for contract and permanent jobs in the hi-tech industries can be found on this site, including all the computing, electronics, aerospace and defence sectors as well as for the users of high technology systems.

Financial Careers Advisers
http://www.financial-careers.co.uk
FCA offers specialist career advice to individuals with respect to employment and jobs in the financial services industry. Investment banking, securities and fund management are the broad areas covered. In particular, it advises on positions within equity and equity derivatives research, sales and trading, corporate finance and equity capital markets, investment management and research, compliance and risk management.

Food Jobs
http://www.foodjobs.co.uk/
Food Jobs is a specialist recruitment consultancy for the food manufacturing and associated industries. It has been successfully recruiting staff for over ten years in a wide range of disciplines. There are links to how to find a job, current vacancies, information about food jobs, links, and more. The numerous vacancies are categorised under such headings as engineers, graduates, production, laboratory, technologists, sales, miscellaneous, quality, planning assurance, and so on.

Graduate Appointments
http://www.gradapps.co.uk
Established in 1963, GA is a specialist London-based recruitment consultancy, part of Megalomedia plc, Lord Saatchi's network of media and new media businesses. It places candidates from recent graduates up to senior level executives into a range of industry sectors such as marketing, PR, sales, new media, IT, research, management consultancy, finance, administration, human resources and customer services. GA says that the positions offered within these industry sectors are as diverse as the clients it recruits for. Once GA has established that it can help you with your job search, you will be invited to a formal and confidential interview with a graduate recruitment consultant at its Covent Garden offices.

Fig. 24. Graduate Appointments.

Graduate Recruitment Bureau

http://www.grb.uk.com

Vacancies for IT, marketing, engineering, finance and science graduates are listed by the employment agency in Sussex. They run an online candidate search service for employers.

Graduate Recruitment Company

http://www.graduate-recruitment.co.uk

GRC are specialists in finding jobs for UK graduates. The site contains a list of current vacancies split into IT and non-IT sections. Jobseekers should fill in the online application form if they want to be added to their database of candidates.

Fig. 25. The Graduate Recruitment Bureau.

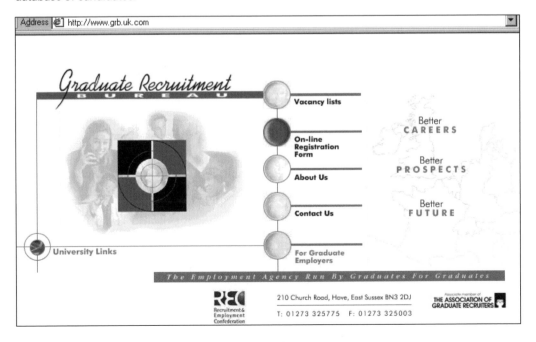

Current vacancies ....

Graduate Recruitment Services
http://www.gradrecruit.co.uk
This south London company features jobs in sales, marketing and the recruitment field.

Graduate Service UK
http://www.recruitgrads.co.uk
This Bedfordshire-based company says: 'We have assisted a high number of graduates into permanent employment in areas such as engineering, IT, finance, administration and leisure but to name a few. We have experienced consultants that can deal in most fields and welcome new graduates or experienced people alike.' Short job descriptions are included with all online vacancies.

Hamilton Recruitment
http://www.hamilton-recruitment.com
Hamilton recruits chartered accountants from the UK and North America to work in the world's premier financial centres such as Bermuda, the Caribbean and the Channel Islands. Here is your chance to earn a tax-free salary and enjoy an outstanding quality of life in these exciting international locations.

Health Professionals
http://www.nursebank.co.uk
This is a recruitment company for nurses who wish to work in London and across the UK. You can find out about contracts, application form, accommodation, the company, training courses, and life in London. The site gives details of registration, work permits, pay scales, accommodation, nursing books, a discussion forum, and nursing links.

High Flyers
http://www.high-flyers.co.uk
Jobs in the City of London and throughout the UK across the financial services trade are offered through this site. They say: 'For experienced, recently trained or graduate candidates we have vacancies with some of the world's biggest and most respected assurance companies, banks, building societies, brokerages, investment houses and financial advisers.'

Independent Insurance Appointments
http://www.indappts.co.uk
These pages offer recruitment services for the UK insurance industry. There are jobs listed online, plus tips for putting together your CV.

IntaPeople
http://www.intapeople.co.uk
IT jobs in the contract and permanent marketplace (mostly in the UK, but a few on mainland Europe as well) are offered through this site.

International Recruitment Consultants
http://www.international-recruitment.co.uk
Check out these web pages for a variety of overseas jobs offering immediate and permanent career opportunities.

Job Security
http://www.jobsecurity.demon.co.uk
Vacancies within the UK security industry are updated daily on this site.

Kestrel Consulting
http://www.peoplesoft-recruitment.com
Kestrel is a global recruitment firm specialising in the recruitment and placement of SAP, Peoplesoft, JD Edwards and client-server experienced professionals throughout the world.

Lateral Solutions
http://www.lateral-solutions.com
Based in Bracknell, Berkshire, Lateral Solutions is part of the Hamilton Parker International group of companies, representing the whole range of recruitment solutions, from executive search to outsourcing. It provides permanent and contract recruitment to the IT, electronic engineering, mobile phone and telecommunications industries worldwide.

LPA Legal Recruitment
http://www.the-lpa.co.uk
This is the web site of a London-based legal recruitment agency which places lawyers at firms throughout the UK and abroad. You can submit your CV online.

Major Players
http://www.majorplayers.co.uk/
Major Players is a London-based marketing and media recruitment agency. You can check out vacancies for sales promotion and multi-disciplined agency staff, design management, new media, creatives, direct

Fig. 26. Major Players has a lively-looking web site for job applicants.

77

marketing, public relations, and secretarial and administrative support. The job details are fairly brief. It also offers a range of graduate trainee positions in various marketing agencies.

Manpower
http://www.manpower.co.uk
The UK's largest employment agency aims to put jobseekers in touch with employers, and vice versa, and to put all sides in touch with their nearest high street branch. This site also has the latest employment news.

Mansell Associates
http://www.mansell.co.uk
This is an agency for technical recruitment of contract and permanent staff at all levels throughout the UK. Its main specialist areas include: mechanical, electrical, electronic and software engineering, computing, plastics and process engineering.

Merrow
http://www.merrow.co.uk/
This consultancy specialises in the recruitment of multi-lingual staff.

Next Wave
http://nextwave.sciencemag.org/
This site provides valuable information for young scientists looking for an alternative to an academic career.

O'Connell Associates
http://www.oconnell.co.uk
O'Connell Associates are recruitment consultants for the financial services sector. O'Connell has links with executive search firms worldwide and lists high-powered vacancies on several continents, along with profiles of individuals in the market for new jobs.

Portman Initial
http://www.portman-initial.co.uk/
Based in the City of London, Portman Initial are recruitment specialists in IT, banking, accountancy, legal, sales and secretarial vacancies. For bankers there may be opportunities in operations staff for FX/derivatives/ treasury/portfolio administration, securities and investment personnel, loans administration and credit analysis, dealers and dealer assistants, senior appointments in all markets and trainee appointments. For accountants there are opportunities for part or fully qualified accountants, derivative product accountants, profit and loss controllers, audit and compliance, accounts administrators including, payroll, ledgers and credit control.

Price Jamieson
http://www.pricejam.com
London-based Price Jamieson handles new media, marketing, communications and healthcare vacancies across the UK, and also in Europe

and the USA. Pricejam Online lists on average 95 per cent of its current assignments, information which is updated every day. If you register with My Pricejam you can store up to ten searches in your profile and then each time you visit you can quickly see only the new jobs that fit your requirements. You can also run these searches on your WAP phone.

Prime Time Recruitment
http://www.primetime.co.uk
Vacancies for technical and engineering staff and sales people are advertised on the site of this recruitment company. There are contact numbers for its offices around England and Wales and an online CV registration service.

Recruiting Solutions
http://www.users.globalnet.co.uk/~recsol/
This is a recruitment agency and consultancy specialising in placing graduates with UK firms. Here it lists services of job seekers and companies and gives links to UK employment sites.

Recruit Media
http://www.recruitmedia.co.uk
Recruit Media deals with freelance and full-time positions in the design and publishing sectors. There are many specialisations within those popular categories, so come here for a browse. The company has offices in Islington and Clerkenwell, London.

INVESTOR IN PEOPLE

Recruitment &
Employment
Confederation

Reed
http://www.reed.co.uk
This is the web site of one of Britain's biggest personnel agencies. It advertises vacancies over a very broad range of categories. They say: 'Register with reed.co.uk and let us find you the right job. Tell us what job you want, attach your CV and we will keep you updated with suitable jobs by email, text message to your mobile phone and WAP.' The site typically has around 39,000 current vacancies on offer.

Reed Graduates
http://www.reed.co.uk/graduate/
'More jobs than any other graduate recruiter' is the Reed boast. Just fill in the registration form and your name comes up whenever a suitable job appears.

Robert Half & Accountemps
http://195.99.180.2/job.html
Robert Half & Accountemps is the largest and longest established (1948) specialist in accountancy and finance recruitment, with 225 offices worldwide. Established in the UK in 1973, it now has 17 regional offices. The company has a global turnover in excess of $1.3 billion. 'Our business is to help people like you gain an edge in the recruitment marketplace whether you're looking for a permanent or temporary position, or just like to keep your options open.'

Current vacancies..

Fig. 27. Reed Graduates.
You can search its
vacancy database and
register for the full range
of services. Visit the Fairs
and go underground to
see Red Mole.

Rosette Recruitment
http://www.rosette.co.uk
This recruitment agency specialises in helping to fill job vacancies for the
hotel and catering industry. Its web site has a directory of hotels with
vacancies around the UK.

Salecareers
http://www.salescareers.co.uk/first.htm
As its name suggests, this recruitment agency specialises in finding
employment for professional sales people (from graduates to account
managers and sales directors) in companies around the UK.

Student Recruitment
http://www.studentrecruitment.com/
If you are a student wanting a potentially tax-free farmworking holiday in
the UK look no further. To qualify, you must be a student in full-time
higher education (college or university) and be under 27 years old.

Time Plan
http://www.timeplan.com/
Click onto this site for a variety of short-term and permanent appointments. There are also loads of curriculum links, links to teaching opportunities abroad and business opportunities for teachers.

Total Systems Resourcing
http://www.tsr.co.uk
Operating out of Cheltenham, this IT recruitment agency has jobs for software engineers, analyst programmers, technical support engineers and
project leaders – both in the UK and abroad. Much of its work is within

the financial sector, including clients within sectors such as investment banking, brokerage and financial point-of-sale systems.

Turns
http://www.turns.net
This company places performing artists in alternative employment between engagements.

 **Specialist Recruitment Agency**

Young Scientist
http://www.young-scientist.co.uk/
Based in Cranleigh, Surrey, this is a specialist recruitment agency for laboratory positions throughout the UK. About half its positions are for candidates seeking their first one or two career appointments. It handles jobs in research and development, technical support and service, quality control and quality assurance, and pilot plant and production. The industries it covers include agrochemicals, biotechnology, chemicals, food and drink, paper and packaging, polymers, pharmaceuticals, toiletries, paints and inks, and specialities. Its services are free and confidential to candidates.

Online vacancy and CV databases

100hot Jobs
http://www.100hot.com/directory/business/jobs.html
As the title says, this site gives you access to the 100 most popular sites related to jobs.

BigBlueDog
http://www.bigbluedog.com
Visit this splendid online service for job seekers, courtesy of the *London Evening Standard*. Sign up here (free) with Big Blue Dog to get an email service of vacancies that suit your 'wish list'. You can also compose a CV on line, and send it off whenever you spot a likely job.

Bio Career
http://www.biocareer.com
The Biotechnology Industry Organisation and SciWeb have combined to develop this online career resource. This site is efficient, effective and an easy way to connect job seekers and recruiters in the biotechnology industry. It provides a service for graduate students, with discussion boards to air workplace issues. You will also find a salary survey, career articles, a BIO career guide, and a web directory with links to sites with career information, scholarships, loans and relocation services.

Current vacancies...

Fig. 28. Big Blue Dog is packed with information and opportunities for graduate job hunters.

BioMedNet Jobs
http://biomednet.com/jobs.htm
This is a London-based worldwide club for the biological and medical community, now part of Reed plc. Its Job Exchange contains nearly 1,000 positions wanted and available in academia and commercial sectors. You can search the jobs database, add your own job advertisement or CV, check out many links to career sites, books and articles, and access other resources to help your job search. You have to complete quite a detailed online application form to register. The site is believed to have in excess of 400,000 subscribers.

Bioscience Jobs
http://www.bioscience-jobs.com
This is an online UK-based confidential CV database for life science graduates. It specialises in employment opportunities in the biomolecular sciences. It welcomes submission of CVs, enquiries about specific posts and requests to advertise job opportunities or search its database of potential candidates. It especially welcomes skills in bioinformatics, 3d structure determination, molecular modelling, protein and peptide chemistry, structural and functional genomics, molecular immunology, and computational chemistry. Job seekers are invited to complete the online form to provide basic details of their qualifications and current experience. The service is mainly seeking candidates with postgraduate experience in industry or basic research.

CareerMosiac.com
http://www.careers.com
CareerMosaic offers job seekers one of the most comprehensive resources for finding a job online while providing companies with a

cost-effective way to reach an expanding market of qualified job candidates.

Daily Mail CareerLink
http://www.peoplebank.com/pb3/candex/CareerLink/CareerLink.htm
This is a free online service: job seekers can register their CVs, which are then available to more than 250 employment agencies all over the UK – and to every employer who uses the internet. You can also search a list of jobs vacant.

Datum Online
http://www.datumeurope.com
Datum has links to big firms advertising their vacancies in the UK, the rest of Europe, USA and the Asia/Pacific rim.

Dice
http://www.dice.com
This is a job search web site for computer professionals, with thousands of high tech permanent, contract, and consulting jobs.

E-CV
http://www.e-cv.com
This US–based company offers to send your resume and cover letter directly to thousands of qualified hiring professionals via electronic networking. Their database consists of over 10,000 hiring companies and professionals.

Film, TV & Commercial Employment Network
http://www.employnow.com
Intended for both beginners and professionals, this site provides information and resources for behind and in front of the camera. There are job listings and industry links.

Financial Times
http://www.ft.com
The City of London's newspaper's web site offers access to mainly senior jobs in accountancy, banking and general finance, IT and other top opportunities.

Gis-a-Job
http://www.gisajob.com
Gis-a-Job has around 70,000 UK job vacancies covering just about all industry sectors. It is free to use. Job seekers' CVs can be distributed to more than 1,000 recruitment agencies in the UK at no charge. You can sign up for its email job alert service.

Graduate Link
http://www.graduatelink.com
Graduate Link operates on behalf of university careers services in Yorkshire and the Humber to promote graduate jobs and careers in the region.

Current vacancies ....

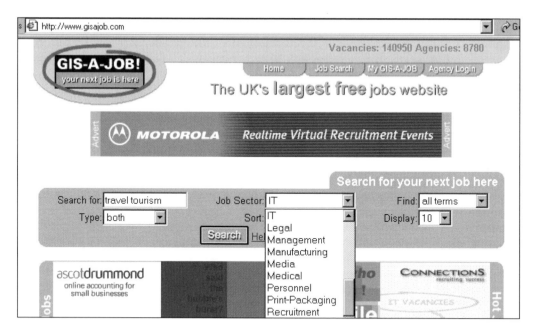

Fig. 29. The web site of Gisajob, an online recruitment information service.

Greythorn
http://www.greythorn.co.uk
This is a searchable database of Australian and UK vacancies, mostly in the IT field.

Guardian
http://www.guardian.co.uk
Through this *Guardian* newspaper site, you can access jobs in IT, science and technology, education, public, health and environment, creative, media, marketing and commercial sectors. There are also appointments for international and graduates jobseekers in both the private and the public sector.

Hong Kong Jobs
http://www.hkjobs.com
This site is dedicated to providing recruitment information in Hong Kong. With access to the largest online database for job openings in the territory, Hong Kong Jobs is capturing a worthwhile share of the growing web audience. The site was substantially relaunched in December 2000.

Inside Careers Guides
http://www.insidecareers.co.uk
From here you can access general recruitment information, current issues and key recruiters in a variety of fields including: engineering, law, patent work, surveying and management consultancy. The site works in partnership with a number of top UK professional bodies such as the Engineering Council, and Institute of Chartered Accountants.

Current vacancies

Internet SourceBook Career Centre
http://www.internetsourcebook.com/jobs/index.html
Here you can explore profiles of more than 500 internet-based companies that are now hiring staff, including links to their recruitment web pages.

IT-pages
http://www.it-pages.co.uk
IT-pages offers IT jobs and careers from recruitment agencies, using a searchable database, plus information, resources, links and various services for people across the IT industry.

JobAsia
http://www.jobasia.com
In JobAsia you have access to three job search engines plus a search wizard to jobs in Hong Kong and other international cities. Jobs are classified into 36 job areas and more than 80 industries. You can save your resume in JobAsia and instantly submit your application online. Check out the company search, bulletin board, education centre, industry profiles and books.

JobFinder
http://www.jobfinder.ie
'Ireland's No.1 career web site' is a searchable file of computing, technical, sales and marketing, finance, medical and administrative vacancies in Northern and Southern Ireland. Tell them about your skills and they will alert you by email if a suitable job crops up.

Job-Hunt
http://www.job-hunt.org
Here you can find thousands of web sites selected and organised to help you in your on-line job search. Explore job leads, newsgroups, agencies, companies, HR sites and online job listings.

Jobmall
http://www.jobmall.co.uk
Here you can find access to thousands of jobs from top recruitment agencies covering IT, education, engineering and the legal professions.

Jobs
http://www.jobs.ac.uk
This is a web site for academic and associated communities where you can link into vacancies and research posts in British universities. You can browse by job discipline or by keywords. The material has been commissioned by the Universities Advertising Group (UAG), a purchasing consortium which consists of 37 universities and institutes of higher education. Around 1,500 vacancies are generally available online.

Getting Started
- How to Use Job-Hunt
- The Riley Guide
- Job Hunters Bible
- Protecting Your Priva

New to the Internet?
- Internet Tutorials

Hot Site of the Week
Ask The Headhunter
ALL Hot Sites by week

For Employers

85

Current vacancies...

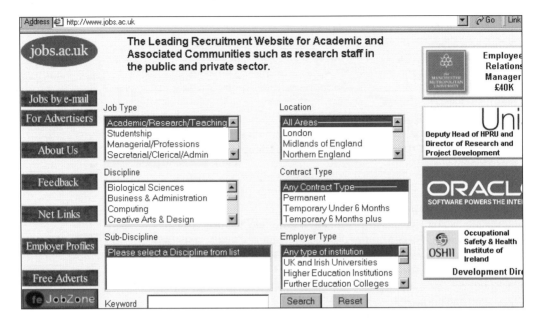

Fig. 30. Jobs.ac.uk is well worth exploring if you are looking for an appointment in academia.

Jobs Bulletin Board
http://www.neptune.u-net.com
These pages have been designed to load quickly and are ideal for offline browsing. You can use the search engines to trawl through jobs in the UK, and employment agencies offering work. You can email your CV to many of them without actually going to their page. A number of sites will send you details of jobs.

Jobserve
http://www.jobserve.com
With around 70,000 vacancies on offer, Jobserve is an established leader in online IT recruitment, having posted vacancies since 1994. It is now regularly used by over 1,800 IT recruitment agencies to advertise more than 150,000 new contract and permanent vacancies every month. If you would like to receive a free daily email message containing the latest vacancies, optionally 'filtered' to your own skills and preferences, you can send a blank email message to: subscribe@jobserve.com.

JobsGoPublic
http://www.jobsgopublic.com
Visit this dedicated site for public sector jobs in the UK, including health, charities, local and central government, housing authorities, and more.

Jobs in Dentistry
http://www.personnelnet.co.uk/jobs-in-health/jobs-in-dentistry/index.htm
You could save yourself time and effort by registering with its free jobs-by-email service. This gives access to one of the largest internet data-bases of healthcare vacancies in the UK. Over 1,500 new jobs are added every month.

Jobs in Pharmacy
http://www.personnelnet.co.uk/jobs-in-health/jobs-in-pharmacy/index.htm

Jobs in Midwifery
http://www.personnelnet.co.uk/jobs-in-health/jobs-in-midwifery/index.htm

Jobs in Physiotherapy
http://www.personnelnet.co.uk/jobs-in-health/jobs-in-physio/index.htm

Jobs in Telecoms
http://www.jobsin.co.uk/telecoms/index.html
Jobs in Telecoms is a specialist recruitment web site for the international telecoms industry. You can find information on permanent, contract and temporary telecoms vacancies throughout the UK and Europe.

Jobsite
http://www.jobsite.co.uk
Here you can search Europe's leading jobs, or register to receive the latest Jobs-by-Email and Jobsite's other award-winning services.

Jobs Network UK
http://www.jobsnetwork.co.uk
Here you can access a large database of jobs advertised on line ranging from administration to validation posts. They say they will email you daily with details of new vacancies.

Jobstop
http://www.jobstop.co.uk
Recruitment consultants on this job site between them advertise literally thousands of jobs. You can select contract, permanent or temporary jobs within a wide range of industries. Jobs of all levels are advertised: all you have to do is select your job category and search. You can narrow your search by subcategory, job location and/or keyword.

Jobs4grads
http://www.jobs4grads.co.uk
This site offers a series of links to graduate job pages on the web (including sites in the USA), universities and sites for potential employers. It was undergoing construction when reviewed.

Jobs Unlimited
http://www.jobsunlimited.co.uk
This is the new, improved job finder from *The Guardian*. There are thousands of jobs and courses to browse: creative, media and sales, secretarial, education, IT, science and technology, public, commercial, international and graduate.

Current vacancies ....

http://www.jobsunlimited.co.uk

The Guardian
The Observer

Go to: Guardian Unlimited home ▾ Go

21.01.2001

Log in

jobsUnlimited

| Home | Media & sales | Education | IT & telecoms | Secretarial | Courses |
| International | Marketing & PR | Public | Sci & tech | New media | Graduates |

Search
Enter a keyword
or phrase

broadcasting   Search   Search tips

More options? Try advanced search

Browse

Browse jobs by sector ▾

Browse recruitment consultancy listings ▾

View selected employer pages

Refresh/reload to see more ads

Fig. 31. Jobs Unlimited is the recruitment web site of *The Guardian* newspaper.

Jobs Worldwide
http://www.jobsworldwide.co.uk
Search for IT jobs worldwide with this UK 'search and selection' agency. It's early days yet, but their database of vacancies should eventually encompass jobs in Australia, New Zealand, Canada, the USA, Europe and the UK.

Jobzone UK
http://www.jobzoneuk.co.uk
You can receive job details by email from leading European companies and recruitment firms.

LGC Net
http://www.lgcnet.com
Visit this site if you want to find out about local authority jobs across England and Wales. Follow the link to LGC Jobs.

London Careers Net
http://www.londoncareers.net
All the jobs on the site are picked from a selection of thousands advertised each week in four London recruitment magazines – *Ms London*, *Midweek*, *Girl About Town* and *Nine to Five*. Select the area of employment you are interested in and you can access a list of the agency site with details of current vacancies. An Overseas Applicants Guide contains information about living and working in London.

Loot: Jobs
http://www.loot.com
Here you will find a large classified advertising database, provided by the popular listing service.

Monster
http://www.monster.co.uk
This is a substantial vacancies database, and part of the global Monster jobs network. When reviewed it contained around 11,000 UK jobs, 26,000 European jobs, and 440,000 global jobs. Features of the site include: My Monster, CV management, a personal job search agent, a careers network, message boards, privacy options, expert advice on job-seeking and career management and free newsletters.

NetJobs
http://www.netjobs.co.uk
This is a big site with a directory made up of about 100 online recruitment agencies and a searchable index of permanent and contract jobs, mostly IT-related.

PeopleBank
http://www.peoplebank.com
This well-established service uses the internet to match employers and employees. It has a database of over 100,000 registered candidates, for whom the service is free.

Portfolio of British Nursing Web Sites
http://www.british-nursing.com
From the home page, you can follow links to hundreds of nursing agencies and other online resources for nurses.

Recruit Online
http://www.recruit-online.co.uk
Recruit Online offers a comprehensive directory of UK recruitment agencies, which you can then search by industry sector. The functional-looking site is updated daily.

Recruitment Scotland
http://www.recruitmentscotland.com
This site lists a diverse range of jobs both inside and outside of Scotland.

Science Online
http://www.sciencemag.org
You can link into scientific job vacancies, research positions, and postings in Europe and the USA under the Professional Network System.

Space Careers
http://www.spacelinks.com/SpaceCareers/
From these home pages, you can access a collection of 200-plus links to place where you can find jobs going in the space and satellite trade.

StepStone
http://www.stepstone.co.uk
Launched in 1996, and with offices in London, StepStone has rapidly grown into one of Europe's leading online recruiting companies, offering one of the largest employment databases on the internet. It offers around

Current vacancies ....

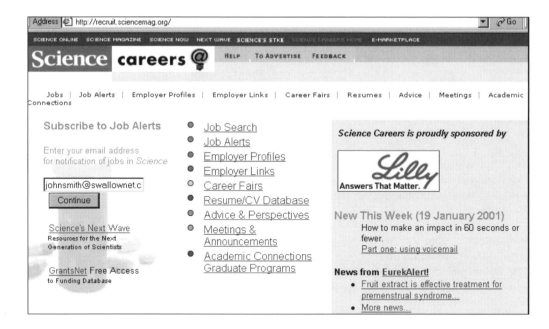

Fig. 32. Science Online could be just the thing, especially if you are thinking of working overseas.

115,000 job vacancies and attracts around 3 million user sessions to the its web sites every month. It has over 420,000 registered subscribers and is used by more than 12,000 companies across Europe. You can search a wide range of occupational categories (Figure 33).

Summer Jobs
http://www.summerjobs.com
Summer Jobs is a database of seasonal and part-time job opportunities. While the primary focus is summer employment for students and education professionals, other jobs may be posted here as well. Jobs are organised by country, state or province, region and city or town. The initial database has a small list of countries and cities that will grow as new jobs are posted. Searching the database may be performed by using keywords or by geographical location.

Taps.com
http://www.taps.com
This is a database of UK and international jobs, with an IT emphasis. It recently announced that Internet Appointments Ltd – the publisher of the Taps.com and Contracts365 recruitment web sites – is being acquired by StepStone.

Teaching and Training Vacancies & Jobsearch
http://www.namss.org.uk/jobs.teach.htm
This is an excellent site offering links to jobsearch guidance and resources plus links to current vacancies in the UK and USA and to various education and training resources.

90

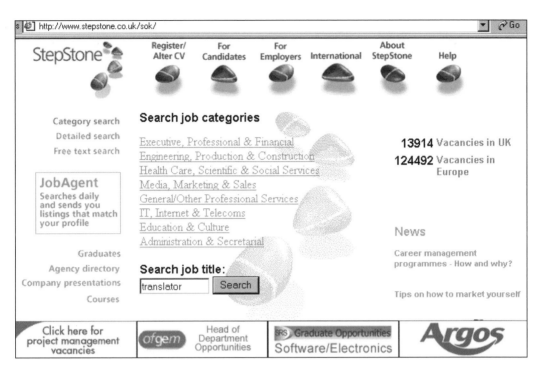

Fig. 33. StepStone, one of the leading European job portal sites.

The Job
http://www.thejob.com
Thousands of jobs from across the UK and Europe are listed in this site. So whether you're experienced, or a graduate searching for your first placement, you should be able to find what you're looking for.

The Times
http://www.the-times.co.uk
Look here for jobs in: accountancy and finance, building and construction, engineering and technical, general appointments, information technology, legal appointments, media, sales and marketing, public appointments and secretarial.

Top Careers
http://www.topcareers.net
With offices in London and Philadelphia, the firm specialises in recruitment and management education. From the home page, you can link into graduate, MBA and executive options. You can register your CV online and have it sent to the top international recruiters worldwide. You can also view profiles from hundreds of graduate employers in its searchable database.

Top Grads
http://www.topgrads.co.uk
They say: 'Top Grads is a service dedicated to graduate opportunities – whether it's the wide array of new opportunities suitable for recent grad-

uates or it's advice and information to succeed – if you're a graduate this is the place to be!' This is a professional-looking service.

Top Jobs
http://www.topjobs.net
This is a comprehensive and constantly updated service which provides listings for Australia, UK, Ireland, Netherlands, Norway, Poland, Sweden, Switzerland, Thailand and the US.

Top Jobs on the Net
http://www.topjobs.co.uk
This is a recruitment site specialising in managerial, professional, technical and graduate jobs. Blue chip firms advertise thousands of jobs here (continually updated). Employer background information and career advice is also on offer. You can search current vacancies by job category.

Fig. 34. Web Recruiters brings together a lot of useful contacts and information in one place.

Web Recruiter Directory
http://www.recruiters.org.uk
This site offers a searchable database of recruitment agencies.

Work Unlimited
http://www.workunlimited.co.uk
There are loads of links to vacancies, careers advice, information and work-related research sites here.

More Internet Handbooks to help you

Finding a Job on the Internet, Brendan Murphy (2nd edition).
Where to Find It on the Internet, Kye Valongo (2nd edition).

6 Graduate employers online

In this chapter we will explore:

▶ *business portal sites*
▶ *private sector employers*
▶ *public sector employers*

. . . .

This chapter provides details of the web sites of a selection of some of the biggest and best-known employer companies and public sector organisations for graduates. You may need some patience while downloading some of their pages. Many of them are heavily loaded with bandwidth-hungry graphics and dynamic content.

Business portal sites

Business Telephone Numbers
http://www.192enquiries.com

BusinessZone
http://www.businesszone.co.uk
This site provides a business information service for home workers and small to medium enterprises providing access to real-time news, company and market research data as well as an accountancy directory and discussion forum.

Companies House
http://www.companies-house.gov.uk
All incorporated companies must be registered at Companies House. The official Companies House web site was launched in 1997 and now receives over 1.4 million page hits per month. It offers free access to a searchable Company Names and Address Index. You can look up information on more than 1.3 million live and recently dissolved companies. Searching for a company can be carried out by using its name or by using its unique company registration number.

Companies Online
http://www.companiesonline.com
Here you will find a substantial Dun and Bradstreet/Lycos directory of American companies, which you can search by state, city, industry and company name. The site also offers links to company web sites.

Company Reports
http://www.corpreports.co.uk
Other useful sources of information on companies are the business news/information providers, where you may be able to find topical snippets of news from the business Corporate Reports.

Graduate employers online..

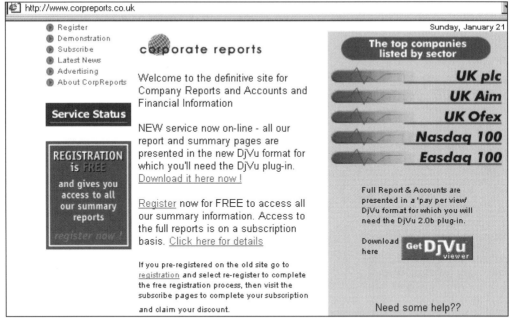

Fig. 35. Corporate Reports is an excellent source of background information about prospective employers, which you can use to impress at interviews and assessments.

Datagold
http://www.datagold.com
On this website, you can find listings of UK companies, searchable by geographic location. Titles include UK Training Directory, UK Recruitment Directory, UK Marketing Directory (actually wider, includes PR, Market Research etc), UK Export Directory, UK Accountants Directory, UK Management Consultants Directory and the UK Internet Service Provider Directory.

Electronic Yellow Pages
http://www.eyp.co.uk/
Here you will find an easy-to-use directory claiming 1.6 million-plus classified businesses around the UK.

Europages Business Directory
http://www.europages.com
This directory offers 500,000 companies selected in 30 European countries. The site is available is several languages.

Europages Link Resources
http://www.webpromotion.co.uk/resourcelinks.htm
Use this site to find complementary companies to target for links. There is a useful facility to look up online businesses sorted by sector.

Federation of Small Businesses
http://www.fsb.org.uk
The FSB is Britain's largest membership organisation for employers, consisting mainly of small and independently owned enterprises.

GET: The Directory of Graduate Recruiters

Fig. 36. Hobsons graduate information service, GET.

http://www.get.hobsons.com

This is an annual publication of the careers specialist, Hobsons, which you can now refer to online. You can link to current vacancies (including international jobs), careers services, professional bodies and distance learning.

Give Me A Job

http://www.givemeajob.co.uk

This is a web site for graduate job seekers. If you are looking for your first job, you will find information about thousands of jobs and careers for graduates. There is plenty of background information about Britain's top employers with hot links to some of them. The site is maintained by the London-based publisher of a series of student guides called On Course Publications.

Hemmington Scott

http://www.hemscott.co.uk

This is a useful and authoritative source of UK company information viewed from the point of view of investment and financial performance.

Internet Directory Enquiries

http://www.internet192.com

Over 1.4 million listings can be accessed through this site which includes an A-Z of business types. You can search by region.

Kompass

http://www.kompass.co.uk

This is a long-established and substantial resource. It maintains a database of more than 180,000 UK manufacturing and service companies.

Graduate employers online...

You can use it to find companies in a specific industry or region.

MarketPlace UK
http://directmarketing.uk.dnb.com/
You can use this site to identify companies by industry and by region.

Monster Research Companies
http://www.changejobs.co.uk/f_grad_3_m.html
Link directly into loads of companies listed in alphabetical order.

The Biz
http://www.thebiz.co.uk
The Business Information Zone is an established online business directory. It contains basic contact details for a whole range of commercial and public sector organisations.

Thomson Directories In Business
http://www.inbusiness.co.uk
A comprehensive online directory of businesses in Britain can be accessed here.

Fig. 37. UK Company News. Here you can explore details of UK quoted companies, a research section and other features.

Trade Association Forum
http://www.martex.co.uk/taf/
This site contains a directory of trade associations. The service is supported by the Department of Trade and Industry and the Confederation of British Industry.

UK Business Net
http://www.ukbusinessnet.com
The site includes information and links for more than 2,000 UK companies online.

UK Business Park Company Search
http://www.andybri.demon.co.uk/
The UK Business Park offers business news in a concise and easy-to-read format. There are three main services: industry news, company search of 1,400 companies over the last two years, and a business news email service a boon for job seekers wanting the latest company background news to help with applications and interviews.

UK Company News
http://www.companynews.co.uk
This is a useful source of financial and other news on specific UK companies. Though targeted primarily at investors, it is means of discovering the current state of health of large and medium-sized PLCs.

Private sector employers

Accenture (formerly Andersen Consulting)
http://www.ac.com
With more than 65,000 people in 48 countries and worldwide revenues of $8.9 billion, Accenture is a force committed to transforming the ecommerce marketplace. Eighty-five of the Fortune Global 100 companies and nearly 75 percent of Fortune's most profitable firms are among its clients. They say: 'By joining our global organisation, you can experience the fun and exhilaration of working across the range of these businesses and share in the wealth created through our mutual success. Together we can change the way the world lives and works.'

Apple Computer
http://www.apple.com/find/sitemap.html
On this site map page, look for the link to job opportunities. Apple says: 'There are a lot of exciting projects at Apple, and we need a lot of talented people to push them forward. We recommend that you search the opportunities that are currently open before applying. Applying for a specific job is the most efficient way to contact us regarding employment.' If you want to send them your resume regarding general employment opportunities at Apple, you can do so here.

Arthur Andersen
http://www.arthurandersen.com
Top international accountancy firm Arthur Andersen says its mission is to build relationships and develop innovative solutions which help dynamic people and organisations create and realise value. The firm is more than 70,000 strong, with 385 offices in 83 countries. From the home page follow the link to careers, where detailed help is available for applicants worldwide.

Graduate employers online...

ASDA
http://www.asda.co.uk
From the top of the home page, follow the link to jobs as ASDA. Their special programme called Flying Start could be your passport to success as an undergraduate. You are also invited to explore a scheme called Talent Store, the name behind a hands-on development programme which can put you in a leading role from day one.

Barclays
http://www.barclays.com
From the home page, follow the link to graduate careers. There are details of summer business placements, and some useful FAQs. They say: 'The graduate programme equips you to reach the most senior positions within your business area or specialist field. Prove that you have the desire and ability to succeed and there are no limits to how far you can go.'

Blue Circle
http://www.bluecircle.co.uk
Blue Circle Industries plc is an international group of heavy building materials companies focused on cement products. Its objective is to create shareholder value through improving margins from its existing businesses, making acquisitions in both mature and high growth developing markets, and integrating its newly acquired assets rapidly and effectively.

Boots
http://www.boots-plc.com
Pharmacy remains the cornerstone of the Boots business in the UK but now, as well as being 'chemists to the nation', it is laying the foundations of a growing range of health and beauty products and related service markets. The firm also has opticians, dentists, chiropodists and offers an expanding range of specialist services to cater for all the diverse wellbeing needs of its customers. From the home page follow the link to career opportunities. There you will find further details of graduate opportunities, MBA opportunities, optometrist opportunities, pharmacist opportunities, and marketing opportunities.

BP
http://www.bpamoco.com
This is the corporate web site of British Petroleum/Amoco. They say: 'This progressive, stimulating business environment demands breakthrough thinking and a pioneering spirit. We need people who can bring fresh ideas and novel approaches to complex operations; people who relish commercial and technological challenges, and have the vision and drive to identify and implement innovative solutions.' You can download an application form from this site.

British Aerospace
http://www.bae.co.uk
British Aerospace and Marconi Electronic Systems have recently

merged into BAE Systems. They are looking for talented and committed people to help develop and deliver total solutions for customers on land, at sea, and in the air. From being the prime contractor for Britain's new nuclear submarine, to making the smallest of gyroscopes, they say, every project will stretch you. They aim to recruit over 900 undergraduates and graduates each year. If you are an engineer with at least two years' work experience you are invited to visit their engineer online recruitment process. From the home page follow the link to recruitment.

British Airways
http://www.britishairwaysjobs.com
This is an excellent example of a corporate recruitment web site, clearly and attractively designed, and with lots of well-signposted information and resources. There are links for example to all about us, training and career development, rewards and benefits, FAQs, career hints and tips, our recruitment centre, give us feedback, and a site guide. There is a vacancy search for everything from customer and cabin services to technical, commercial and operational careers, a flight simulator, and many other interesting features.

British Energy
http://www.british-energy.co.uk
British Energy is one of the UK's largest electricity companies has around 20 per cent of the generation market, and a developing generation business in the United States. It was the first nuclear utility to be privatised and operating in a fully competitive market. From the home page follow the link to recruitment, 'Switched On'. They say: 'With the challenges we face and the opportunities we are looking to exploit, technically and commercially our new recruits must be more switched on than ever before.'

British Nuclear Fuels
http://www.bnfl.com
British Nuclear Fuels provides products and expertise to the nuclear energy industry worldwide. Its business covers fuel manufacture and reactor services, electricity generation, spent fuel management and nuclear decommissioning and clean up. From the home page follow the link to career opportunities. The company employs around 23,000 people worldwide, and recruits about 50 to 90 new graduates each year.

Cable & Wireless
http://www.cableandwireless.com
From its beginning in the 1860s, Cable & Wireless has played a big part in the establishment and development of telecommunications around the world. Its web site is illustrated with material from its collections of photography, film and original documents. From the home page follow the link to jobs. These are categorised as UK jobs, contract assignments, and international opportunities. To apply for positions with Cable & Wireless in the UK you must be a British or EU passport holder, or hold a visa permitting you to live and work in the UK. They say that CVs should be formatted in Word 7 (Windows 95).

Graduate employers online..

Cadbury
http://www.cadbury.co.uk
'All you ever needed to know about chocolate... on the web!' As market leader of chocolate confectionery in the UK, Cadbury's brand portfolio includes Cadbury's Dairy Milk, the undisputed leader in block chocolate, and Cadbury's Roses, the UK's top selling assortment together with such famous brands as Cadbury's Flake, Wispa, and TimeOut. From the automatically loading popup window, follow the link to recruitment. They say: 'Get your career off to a cracking start! Here at Cadbury, we've developed a merchandising development programme that will provide you with the ideal start to a career in sales and merchandising.'

Citibank
http://www.citibank.com
Citibank is one of the world's largest financial services groups, whose interests include Citibanking, private banking, cards, consumer finance, life insurance and personal property casualty insurance. From the home page follow the link to careers. The site features some very stylish graphics.

Corus Group (formerly British Steel)
http://www.corusgroup.com
Corus is a major European producer of steel and aluminium, the result of a merger in 1999 between British Steel and Koninklijke Hoogovens. Everything we use in our daily lives has in some way involved metal in its creation. Corus works with automotive and packaging designers, architects, engineers, and people engaged in product and industrial design. From the home page follow the link to working for Corus. They say: 'Working for Corus in an innovative and technology-driven environment is never dull. Initiative, innovation, teamwork and leadership are some of the key qualities we look for. Specific vacancies range from staff to senior management and are grouped by country of origin. We also have a requirement for a graduate intake of approximately 375 per annum. Apply online today!'

Disney
http://www.disney.com/disneycareers/index.html
Disney is probably the world's best-known brand of children's entertainment, whose activities range from film-making to leisure resorts and vacations. It has an enormous and very breezily presented web site. Each of the positions on the Disney Careers site is posted by one of the many companies, divisions, and departments that together make up the Disney organisation. To learn more about a particular business, select from the list of business activities, which are grouped according to the human resources offices with which they are associated.

Dresdner Kleinwort Benson
http://main.dresdnerkb.com
From the DKB home page follow the link to careers. They say: 'At Dresdner Kleinwort Benson, we recruit energetic, career driven professionals at

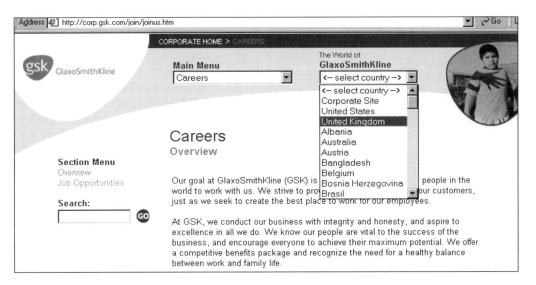

various stages of their academic or working lives, into roles based in London, Frankfurt, New York, Tokyo and Hong Kong. If you are currently studying for, or have recently completed your studies either at graduate, postgraduate or MBA level, please read on to see if our career opportunities match your aspirations.'

Fig. 38. At the end of 2000, Glaxo Wellcome and SmithKline Beecham agreed the terms of a merger to form a new pharmaceuticals giant GlaxoSmithKline (GSK).

Glaxo Smith Kline
http://corp.gsk.com
Glaxo Smith Kline is a leading UK-based international research-based company committed to fighting disease by bringing innovative medicines and services to patients throughout the world and to the healthcare providers who serve them. They say: 'We know our people are vital to the success of the business; we encourage everyone to achieve their maximum potential. We value diversity and each other's individual contribution; we encourage mutual trust and respect.' The company has requirements for new graduates and for people with experience in manufacturing and supply, IS, research and development, and commercial areas. You can click on each area to find out more or to view a selection of current vacancies.

Hewlett Packard Europe
http://www.jobs.hp.com
Founded in 1939 and based in Palo Alto, California, Hewlett Packard today has 86,000 employees worldwide. There are more than 600 sales and support offices and distributorships in 120 countries. You can search for current employment opportunities with Hewlett-Packard by specifying selection criteria (including region) here on the careers section of its vast web site.

Honeywell
http://www.honeywell.com
From the home page follow the link to careers. From there, there are links

Search

databases

All IBM ▾ Go

→ Advanced searc

Jobs at IBM

Related links:

Jobs worldwide

→ IBM Worldwide

to find a job, submit a resume, build a resume, recruiting events, on campus, meet our people, and learn our culture.

IBM

http://www.ibm.com

IBM aims to lead in the creation, development and manufacture of the industry's most advanced information technologies, including computer systems, software, networking systems, storage devices and microelectronics. Its worldwide network of IBM solutions and services professionals translates these advanced technologies into business value for its customers. From the home page follow the link to job seekers, where more detailed help can be found.

ICI

http://www.ici.com

ICI is a world leader in the manufacture and distribution of industrial chemicals, paints and allied products. From the home page follow the link to graduate recruitment. This offers insights into its global business, details of training and development, and application procedures, together with profiles. There is an applicant-friendly FAQ section that deals with such issues as: What does the recruitment process entail? If I receive a job offer but I still have lots of questions to ask about the job, will I get a chance to come back to someone before making my decision?

Intel

http://www.intel.com

Intel is one of the world's most successful manufacturers of computer microprocessors, notably the Pentium chip used in millions of personal computers worldwide. From the home page follow the link to company information, then jobs. This is a substantial area of the Intel web site, with its own site map, and links to other Intel web sites around the world.

ITN

http://www.itn.co.uk

ITN is the news provider for the three commercial channels in Britain: ITV, Channel 4 and Channel 5. ITN began broadcasting the world's first convergent multimedia news channel on digital satellite, cable and terrestrial television in 2000. ITN New Media is the leading producer of customised digital news and information services for the converging media market and produces the ITN website itn.co.uk.

KPMG

http://www.kpmg.co.uk/uk/career

KPMG is a global firm providing accountancy and management consultancy services to business and private clients in 159 countries. They say: 'We are the largest professional firm of business advisors in Europe, and one of the largest in the world. We offer a stimulating working environment working with our wide portfolio of clients. Our staff work in industry focused teams covering a wide range of disciplines.' The careers section of its web site is very clear and comprehensive.

Legal and General Assurance
http://www.legal-and-general.co.uk

Lego
http://www.lego.com

Logica
http://www.logica.com
Logica says that its mission is to help leading organisations worldwide achieve their business objectives through the innovative use of information technology. The site has a dedicated careers area, with dropdown menus and links to help you navigate job opportunities in locations worldwide.

Marks and Spencer
http://www.marks-and-spencer.co.uk
Marks and Spencer is Britain's biggest and best-known chain of clothing shops and high street stores, struggling in recent years against new competitive pressures and changes in the retail marketplace.

Microsoft
http://www.microsoft.com/jobs
This is a large and clearly organised area of the gigantic Microsoft web site. You will find all you want to know about possible career paths with the company, life inside Microsoft, global locations, its people, vision and products. They say: 'Microsoft's vision is to empower people through great software – any time, any place and on any device.'

Motorola
http://www.mot.com
Motorola is a global leader in providing integrated communications and embedded electronic solutions. This includes everything from software-enhanced wireless telephone to messaging and satellite communications products and systems, and set-top terminals for broadband cable television operators. On the home page look for the section on Corporate Information, then follow the link to employment.

Nestle UK
http://www.nestle.com
With a total workforce of around 230,000 people in some 500 factories worldwide, Nestlé is not only Switzerland's largest industrial company, but it is also the world's largest food company. Nestlé products are available in nearly every country around the world.

Norwich Union Insurance
http://www.norwich-union.co.uk
With over £200 billion of assets under management, and more than 15 million customers worldwide, Norwich Union and its new partner CGU is one of Britain's biggest financial services companies. They say: 'If you have the skills and motivation to play a major part in our future, then we

Graduate employers online...

can offer you excellent career prospects, a competitive salary package and professional training. From the home page follow the link to jobs, which are arranged under IT vacancies and general vacancies.

Ogilvy
http://www.ogilvy.com
Ogilvy & Mather is one of the top names in brand development, marketing and advertising. They say: 'It is our job to create, nurture and sustain our clients' brands through all media and markets. We accomplish this through the philosophy and practice of brand stewardship – a proprietary set of tools and techniques to understand, develop and enhance the relationship consumers have with a brand.' The web site includes a worldwide office locator.

the people
perspective ■
management
development
calendar ■
applying ■
graduate
opportunities ■

Pearson
http://www.pearson.com
Pearson is an international media company. It employs more than 25,000 people in 50 countries worldwide, and has millions of customers. It has major interests in education, business information and consumer publishing. The slogan of this old-established and ambitious international publishing and media group is 'great content in any media.' The company's main operating divisions include education (Pearson Education), book publishing (Penguin Books) and newspaper publishing (*The Financial Times*). From the home page follow the link to people, then to graduate opportunities.

Pirelli
http://www.pirelli.com/web/site/default.htm
The origins of this famous tyre company date back to 1872, when Giovanni Batista Pirelli began to manufacture and sell elastic rubber products. Today, the company is also at the forefront of cable and superconductor technology. On the home page, use the dropdown search menu and select jobseeker. This in turn gives you a menu of: working with us, functional areas, target jobs, learning with us, supporting your performance, supporting your growth, supporting your know-how, growing with us, our tools, our programmes, CV, and application form.

Powergen
http://www.pgen.com
Powergen is the UK's leading integrated gas and electricity company. They say: 'Our vision is to create one of the world's leading independent electricity and gas businesses. We aim to grow by generating, distributing and supplying power both in the UK and other countries in which we operate. As a low-cost, innovative and environmentally responsible operator, we deliver value and quality to our customers, shareholders, employees, partners and communities.' From the home page follow the link to jobs. Here you can search for current job vacancies within the Powergen group, create your own CV and apply for jobs online.

Price Waterhouse Coopers

http://www.pwcglobal.com

PWC is one of the world's biggest and most prestigious accountancy and auditing groups, with 150,000 employees in 850 offices in 150 countries. They say: 'Most of our clients operate in specific industries, each with its own characteristics, cycles and needs. For maximum effectiveness, we have organized ourselves likewise. Worldwide, industry-specialised cross-disciplinary teams deliver services to clients in 22 defined industries.' From the home page follow the link to worldwide careers.

Proctor & Gamble

http://www.pg.com

Proctor & Gamble is one of the world's biggest producers, marketers and distributors of family care, household and personal care products. This is naturally a very consumer-oriented site, though it does include plenty of information about job opportunities as well. On the home page, follow the link to jobs. This produces further links to topics such as apply now, job opportunities, current job postings, internships, succeeding at P & G, the application process, college recruiting, lifestyle and benefits, and FAQs.

Prudential

http://www.prudential.co.uk

Through its businesses in Europe, the US and Asia, the Pru provides a broad range of retail financial products and services, and fund management, to millions of customers worldwide. The company has been established for 150 years. On the home page follow the link to Join Us. They say: 'Prudential is a diverse organisation and therefore offers a variety of career opportunity levels. We intend to develop this aspect of our web site for careers in the future. In the meantime, most vacancies are advertised in either the national or local trade journals.' The site does however contain details of its Fast Track Development Programme, designed for people with 4 to 7 years' commercial experience who are looking for a career in general management.

Railtrack

http://www.railtrack.co.uk

Under relentless scrutiny from politicians, the public and the media, Railtrack faces some considerable business and technological challenges. If you feel you have the qualities to make a positive contribution in such an environment, explore the site map, and under corporate information follow the link to graduate recruitment. The company offers a fast-track training scheme to provide the skills to equip applicants to make rapid progress in general management, electrical and mechanical engineering, and civil engineering.

Reuters

http://www.reuters.com/careers/graduate/

Reuters is a premier global news and information service. It says it has

Graduate employers online...

Address 🔲 http://about.reuters.com/careers/graduate/index.asp ▼ 🔗 Go | Link

REUTERS ⏺ Graduate Opportunities   About Reuters

Home | Who are we? | What do we offer? | Applying | Help yourself | Contact us

Who are we?
Reuters in reality - take a look at a world leader in action.

What do we offer?
Find out about everything from management training to internships.

Applying
Find out about our application process, and the online application form.

Help yourself
Get career advice, CV tips, download goodies etc..

Index... ▼

It's Here

The Company - financial markets, multimedia news, integrity, Internet, opportunity, more...

The Opportunity - Challenge, variety, international, bright people, great future, more...

Recruitment NEWS:

e-Apprenticeship Scheme
If you've graduated, an exciting opportunity.

More...
(posted 16 Jan)

It's Now

Look into your future. Great places, interesting people, challenge and

Lighten up! Brilliant images - Cute, Crazy World, Sport. New

Dot com to wireless, Incubator to Greenhouse, networks to

Events drive markets! Feel the buzz! Taste the excitement. Reuters

Fig. 39. Reuters is at the forefront of the global media revolution, and could form a great starting point for your career in the world of information.

some neat and innovative projects which put the company at the cutting edge of the e-world, with brand new products, investments in start-ups, portals, joint ventures and a mission to 'make the financial markets really work on the internet'. From this page you can find out about everything from management training to internships, explore the Reuters application process, and complete an online application form.

Rolls Royce
http://www.rolls-royce.com
Rolls Royce is a blue-chip engineering company, with an established reputation in civil aerospace, defence aerospace, and marine and industrial engineering. It is a world leader in gas turbine technology. On the home page, follow the link to careers. They say: 'Only world-class people can deliver the world's best service. We require our people not only to be skilled in their jobs, but also to understand the wider commercial implications of what they do and to be motivated to make the greatest possible contribution.'

Safeway Stores
http://www.safeway.co.uk/about/careers/
They say: 'If you are a graduate and are interested in a job at Safeway, then these pages are definitely for you – find out more about the Think graduate programme.' For information about Safeway plc, including press releases, annual reports and accounts, you can use the link provided to visit the company's corporate pages.

Sainsbury
http://www.sainsbury.co.uk
Sainsbury's Supermarkets is a leading UK food-retailing business, first

established in 1869. Today, it operates from about 430 stores selling over 23,000 products of which 40 per cent are own brand. With its slogan 'Making life taste better' the company employs over 138,000 people serving around 10 million customers per week. On the home page, follow the link to Join Us, where you can find out about graduate, in-store and management opportunities

Schering Health Care
http://www.schering.co.uk
SHCL is a subsidiary of SAG, an international research-based pharma-ceutical company based in Berlin. The company is part of a global business which develops new products in female healthcare, diagnos-tics, therapeutics and dermatology. Operating from offices in Burgess Hill, West Sussex, it is responsible for the clinical development, marketing and distribution of the Schering range of pharmaceuticals in the United Kingdom. On the home page, follow the link to Employment Opportu-nities. The site includes some careers guidance and a jobs database covering medical, marketing and management careers.

Go to jobs databas

Past to Future

Careers

Business Areas

Corporate Profile

Schering in the UK

How to find us

Scottish Power
http://www.scottishpower.plc.uk
Scottish Power supplies energy to millions of business and domestic customers across the UK and the western United States. Its sales total around £6 billion. In its ten years since privatisation the company has seen significant organic growth as well as key acquisitions in the UK and US utility sectors. It offers a broad range of utilities, spanning gas, electricity and water services to more than 5 million homes in the UK, and internet and telecom services throughout its majority owned subsidiary, Thus. US activities involve generation, distribution and supply of electri-city. On the home page, follow the link to careers.

Shell International Petroleum
http://www.shell.com/home/
Shell's core businesses compass exploration, production, chemicals, gas and power, oil products, and renewables, and a surprisingly diverse range of other business operations. This is a gigantic global energy busi-ness, with an online presence to match. A dropdown menu will lead you to a large number of other Shell sites around the world.

SmithKline Beecham
http://www.sb.com
SmithKline Beecham is one of the world's leading healthcare companies. It discovers, develops, manufactures and markets pharmaceuticals, vac-cines, over-the-counter medicines and all kinds of health-related consumer products. It markets over 400 branded products, and employs 47,300 people worldwide with operations in 160 countries. On the home page, follow the link to careers. Job postings are updated weekly. The company recently merged with Glaxo Wellcome.

Graduate employers online...

Sony
http://www.sony.com/SCA/job.html
Sony is a top manufacturer of audio, video, communications and information technology products for both consumer and professional markets. Its music, motion pictures, TV production, computer entertainment operations and online businesses make it one of the most comprehensive entertainment companies in the world. Sony offers numerous opportunities in its various operating divisions and companies. Current job vacancies are posted by each individual Sony company on its own web site.

Tesco
http://www.tesco.com/recruitment/html/index.htm
Tesco is the UK's number one food retailer. An ambitious multinational organisation turning over more than £20 billion a year, it is focused today on becoming a leading global retailer and a world-class business. By 2002 it expects to have around 650 stores in the UK, and a further 120 in central Europe Asia. This web page deals with graduate recruitment at Tesco. It includes company information, graduate departments, and details of the selection process. A noticeboard contains news of university careers fairs that Tesco will be attending.

Unigate Graduate Recruitment
http://www.unigate.plc.uk/recruit/index.htm
This site offering training for graduates plus how to apply for production, engineering, finance, commercial, distribution, R&D, IT and general management positions.

Unilever
http://www.ucmds.com
Some 250,000 Unilever employees generate £27 billion sales each year. Around the world, its foods, home and personal care brands are chosen by millions of consumers each day. With operations in more than 90 countries, this is a truly global business but one that is managed locally – a structure that gives its managers the space they need to lead and innovate. Local operating companies have the responsibility for earning customers' trust and meeting their needs. The well-organised careers section of the site includes the latest recruitment information, a set of helpful FAQs, and online application form.

Unipart International Graduate Recruitment
http://graduate.unipart.co.uk
The international marketing and sales arm of the car parts company explain their programme for recruiting and training university graduates for a career with the company. They invite applications for the programme or industrial placements online.

United Biscuits Graduate Resourcing
http://www.ubgraduates.com
Managerial information for jobs on offer with this huge UK-based com-

pany (products include Jaffa Cakes and Hobnobs) who already employ 20,000 people around the world.

Vickers Defence Systems

http://www.vickersdefence.co.uk

VDS is a world leader in integrated high technology land defence systems. Its expertise embraces products and services that include armoured vehicles and sub-systems, training and simulation, bridging, logistic support, systems integration and proof and experimental ranges. On the home page, follow the link to careers. The company is part of Rolls Royce.

Vodafone

http://www.vodafone.co.uk

A staggering one in six people in the UK now owns a Vodafone, and in a short space of time the company has become the biggest in the FTSE index of leading quoted companies. On the home page, follow the link to careers. To search for a job you can then access a vacancy database. If there are currently no suitable vacancies, you can tell Vodafone what your perfect job would be and they say they will tell you when a suitable opportunity arises. The company also runs a graduate programme at:

Fig. 40. In just a few years, Vodafone has established itself as one of the most valuable FTSE companies.

www.vodafone.co.uk/graduates

Whitbread

http://www.whitbread.co.uk

They say: 'Whitbread is a blend of 90,000 people and many household brand names With so many big name brands supported by a number of strong, well-established central resources, we offer a full range of careers across the entire leisure industry.' On the home page, follow the link to recruitment.

Graduate employers online...

WH Smith
http://www.whsmith.co.uk
WHSmith is one of the UK's largest and best established retailers, with over 500 high street, airport, and railway station stores selling stationery, newspapers, magazines, books, and a whole lot more. It operates a graduate recruitment scheme. For details of this see:

> http://www.whsmith-recruitment.co.uk

Wimpey Construction
http://www.wimpey.co.uk/corporate/gradtra.html
George Wimpey plc is the UK's largest home building group. The company has been in operation for 120 years and operates throughout the UK and America. The group has three operating brands: Wimpey Homes and McLean Homes in the UK, and Morrison Homes in the USA. Group turnover is around £1,400 million a year. They say: 'For our continued success we are building a small and exclusive cadre from which our future senior management will be drawn. The training scheme will cover all aspects of the business including four key functions of production, finance, sales and marketing and land.'

Public sector employers

Civil Service
http://www.civil-service.gov.uk/jobs/home/index.asp
Government today employs an enormous number and range of people, and there are opportunities for almost everyone. The Civil Service runs many different types of recruitment schemes, some organised centrally and some by central management units. Most are run by individual government departments and agencies. On this web site you can discover how to use your own particular specialism, explore the wide range of career opportunities available, view a list of current vacancies by region, and check out forthcoming careers fairs.

Fig. 41. The UK Civil Service recruitment gateway leads to a diverse array of state employment possibilities.

Address | http://www.civil-service.gov.uk

UK Home Civil Service
The Civil Service for the 21st Century

Welcome to the Civil Service Web Site here you will find links to :

Civil Service Reform
Creating a Civil Service for the 21st Century.

Civil Service Recruitment Gateway
Your direct route for working in government.

Current Vacancies in the Civil Service
Current vacancies by region.

Fast Stream European and Recruitment
Promotes recruitment to the UK Civil Service Fast Stream Development Programme,
and representation of UK candidates in posts in the European Union.

HM Prison Service
http://www.hmprisonservice.gov.uk/
In the prison service today, around 60,000 inmates (and rising) are contained by a staff of 40,000. To explore career opportunities in the service, go from the home page to the site map, and look for corporate information/recruitment. There you will find details of employment opportunities within the prison service for fast track entry as a prison governor and details of the application process for prison officers. The service as a whole faces some big management and cultural challenges.

Ministry of Defence
http://www.mod.uk
The MOD is responsible for the Army, Royal Navy and Royal Air Force, and for civilians involved with defence work. From the home page follow the link to careers, where information is shown separately for each branch of the armed forces. As Britain's largest employer, the Army offers more than 15,000 vacancies annually for people of all ages, abilities and educational standards. All branches of the services offer considerable variety of opportunity, the chance to learn valuable skills, to travel, and enjoy a strong community and team spirit.

Police Services
http://www.police.uk
On the home page, follow the links to the individual regional police forces for details about recruitment in local areas.

Post Office Hot Spot
http://www.hot-spot.co.uk
The modern Post Office is an energetic and increasingly commercially focused organisation. Its business include the Royal Mail, Post Office Counters, Parcelforce Worldwide, and Subscription Services. It has been given greater commercial freedom to enter new markets and make partnerships with complementary businesses. It needs people who can drive forward its change programmes and provide leadership to its people. Check out details of its Careers in Business Management programmes.

More Internet handbooks to help you

Finding a Job on the Internet, Brendan Murphy.
Where to Find It on the Internet, Kye Valongo (2nd edition).

7 Industry-specific contacts

In this chapter we will explore:

▶ *national training organisations*
▶ *professional bodies*
▶ *professional and trade journals*
▶ *other useful contacts*

. . . .

National training organisations

▶ *National Training Organisations* – NTOs are industry-led agencies responsible for the promotion of learning, skills, training and development issues relating to their employment sectors. A good jumping-off point is the NTO National Council's own web site, which contains an NTO finder: http://www.nto-nc.org

Banking and Building Societies NTO
http://www.bbsnto.org

Board for Education and Training in the Water Industry
http://www.betwi.demon.co.uk/noframe.htm
BETWI was established in 1992 to act as NTO and lead body for the UK water sector. It has the key responsibility for developing education and training arrangements in the water sector.

Fig. 42. National Training Organisations (NTOs).

British Ports Industry Training
http://www.bpit.co.uk
From this page you can search for employers in the area of the UK in which you would like to work. You will find a list of most of the jobs in the ports industry.

Community Justice NTO
http://www.communityjusticento.co.uk/index.html
The CJNTO promotes training and development for people in professions involved with crime prevention and working with offenders and victims of crime, such as police, probation staff, community volunteers and council workers.

Construction Industry Training Board
http://www.citb.org.uk
Did you know that one in 14 working people is in the construction business? A lot of people will benefit from the CITB's online guide to career options, training, qualifications, health and safety, learning resources and more.

Cultural Heritage NTO
http://www.chnto.co.uk

Electricity Training Association
http://www.eta.org.uk

Electronics and Software Services NTO
http://www.ess.org.uk

Engineering Construction ITB
http://www.ecitb.org.uk

Engineering and Marine Training Authority
http://www.emta.org.uk

Food and Drink NTO
http://www.foodandrinknto.org.uk

Gas Industry NTO
http://www.ginto.co.uk

Glass Training Limited
http://www.glasstrg.demon.co.uk

Hospitality Training Foundation
http://www.htf.org.uk

Insurance and Related Financial Services NTO
http://www.cii.co.uk/nto.htm

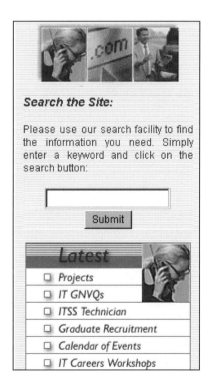

Search the Site:

Please use our search facility to find the information you need. Simply enter a keyword and click on the search button:

[   ]

Submit

Latest

❑ Projects
❑ IT GNVQs
❑ ITSS Technician
❑ Graduate Recruitment
❑ Calendar of Events
❑ IT Careers Workshops

Industry-specific contacts...

Home

Contact Lantra

Lantra & the environment

Qualifications & training

Lantra National Organisation Training
http://www.eto.co.uk
This site is aimed at everyone who is interested in environmental conservation, skills, education, jobs, careers, work and training, including students, volunteers and employees, employers and training and education providers. Click onto N/SVQs, national traineeships and modern apprenticeships.

Local Government NTO
http://www.lgmb.gov.uk

Management and Enterprise NTO
http://www.meto.org.uk

Metier
http://www.metier.org.uk
The NTO for the arts and entertainment industries provides career advice and information about qualifications both for aspiring performers and for those who want to work behind the scenes.

Motor Industry Training Council
http://www.mitc.co.uk

National Council for Training of Journalists
http://www.itecharlow.co.uk/nctj/
This is site offers advice on careers and training in journalism.

Pharmaceutical Industry NTO
http://www.abpi.org.uk

Print and Graphic Communication NTO
http://www.bpif.org.uk

Science, Technology and Mathematics Council
http://www.stmc.org.uk

Security Industry Training Organisation
http://www.sito.co.uk
SITO is a leading provider of qualifications for the security industry. You can link into news, conferences, standards, training, qualifications, projects and links.

SETNET
http://www.setnet.org.uk
This is a site for the Science Engineering Technology Mathematics Network, a joint venture for telling UK teachers, business and industry about science, engineering, technology and maths-related schemes and initiatives.

Skillset
http://www.skillset.org
This is the NTO for broadcast, film, video and multimedia.

Sports and Recreation NTO
http://www.sprito.org.uk

Teacher Training Agency
http://www.teach-tta.gov.uk/index.htm

Travel Training Company
http://www.tttc.co.uk
The Travel Training Company is the principal provider of training and qualifications for anybody looking for a career in travel or already working
within the travel industry.

Professional bodies

Advertising Association
http://www.adassoc.org.uk

Art Libraries Society UK & Ireland
http://arlis.nal.vam.ac.uk
This site includes a career section.

Association of Chartered Certified Accountants
http://www.acca.org.uk

Association of Chartered Accountants in England & Wales
http://www.icaew.co.uk

Association of Corporate Treasurers
http://www.corporate-treasurers.co.uk

Association of International Accountants
http://www.a-i-a.org.uk
A Vacancies Board brings you details of the latest job opportunities, in
association with StepStone.

British Association for Counselling
http://www.bac.co.uk

British Psychological Society
http://www.bps.org.uk

British Computer Society
http://www.bcs.org.uk
From the home page, you can access general computing career information.

Industry-specific contacts..

British Institute of Professional Photography
http://www.bipp.com
The careers section has good coverage of specialist work areas.

British Medical Journal
http://www.bmj.com/
Follow the main link to Jobs, Courses, and Careers.

British Phonographic Industry
http://www.bpi.co.uk
Visit this site for their careers section and links to record labels.

British Society for Immunology
http://www.immunology.org
On this site, you can access vacancy listings, postgraduate course information and studentships.

Broadcast Journalism Training Council
http://www.bjtc.org.uk

Chartered Accountancy Student Society of London
http://www.cassl.com

Chartered Institute of Banking
http://www.cib-org.uk

Chartered Institute of Management Accountants
http://www.cima.org.uk

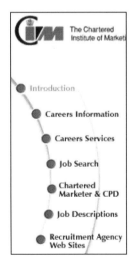

Chartered Institute of Marketing
http://www.cim.co.uk
Visit this site for a useful career section plus application advice.

Chartered Institute of Personnel & Development
http://www.cipd.co.uk

Chartered Institute of Public Finance Accountants
http://www.cipfa.org.uk

Chartered Insurance Institute
http://www.cii.co.uk

Chartered Institute of Purchasing & Supply
http://www.cips.org
There are vacancy listings and useful links to careers in purchasing & supply through this home page.

Design and Technology Association
http://www.data.org.uk
DATA is the recognised professional association which represents all

those involved in design and technology education. You can link into publications, resources, recruitment, conferences and contacts.

Engineering Council
http://www.ce500.co.uk
Check here for graduate vacancies in engineering consultancies.

Incorporated Society of Musicians
http://www.ism.org
This site maintains a good careers section and useful links.

Incorporated Society of Valuers and Auctioneers
http://www.homes-on-line.com/isva/
Look here for profiles of careers in commercial and residential property.

Institute of Biomedical Science
http://www.ibms.org
From this homepage, you can explore career publications and a list of accredited postgraduate and top-up courses.

Institute of Chartered Accountancy in Scotland
http://www.icas.org.uk

Institution of Chemical Engineers
http://www.icheme.org
You can link into vacancies and general career information. They say 'It's a blast.' You will need the Macromedia Flash Player.

Institution of Civil Engineers
http://www.ice.org.uk
Look here for vacancies, careers advice and companies approved for training.

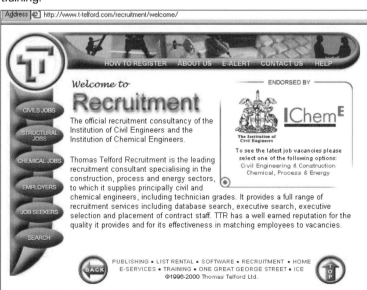

Fig. 43. Thomas Telford Recruitment is the official recruitment consultancy of the Institution of Civil Engineers and the Institution of Chemical Engineers.

Industry-specific contacts...

Institute of Investment Management and Research
http://www.iimr.org.uk
The IIMR is the professional body providing qualifications for the profession of investment analysts and fund management.

Institute of Leisure & Amenity Management
http://www.ilam.co.uk
You can link into some useful addresses through this site and download some free careers information.

Institute of Linguistics
http://www.iol.org.uk
You can link into vacancy listings and information on qualifications.

Latest News
Management Qua
Management Dev
IM's Branches
Public Affairs
Press Information
Special Interest G

Institute of Management
http://www.inst-mgt.org.uk
The site tells you about its management qualifications, membership, and career development.

Institute of Physics and Engineering in Medicine
http://www.ipem.org.uk
This home page will give you access to careers information and vacancy listings.

Institute of Practitioners in Advertising
http://www.ipa.co.uk

Institute of Public Relations
http://www.ipr.org.uk
This site maintains a careers section with details of graduate schemes and placements.

Institute of Translation & Interpreting
http://www.iti.org.uk

Law Society
http://www.lawsociety.org.uk
The site includes details of training courses for solicitors and trainee solicitors.

Library Association
http://www.la-hq.org.uk
Check here for information on training for work in librarianship or information science.

Physiological Society
http://www.physoc.org
Here you can access vacancy listings, PhD opportunities and links to careers pages.

Royal Aeronautical Society
http://www.raes.org.uk
This site offers a great careers section plus lists of associated companies and funding.

Royal Institution of Chartered Surveyors
http://www.rics.org.uk/
From the home page, you can access careers information about the work of surveyors, and search a database of surveyors by specialism.

Royal Pharmaceutical Society of Great Britain
http://www.rspgb.org.uk

Royal Town Planning Institute
http://www.rtpi.org.uk
The RTPI is the professional body and registered charity that works to maintain and improve standards in town planning. It accredits university courses. It provides information on careers in town and country planning.

Society for General Microbiology
http://www.socgenmicrobiol.org.uk
This site offers advice for graduates plus information about postgraduate courses, funding and studentships.

University Council for Education of Teachers
http://www.ucet.ac.uk.org.uk

Professional and trade journals

Accountancy
http://www.accountancymag.co.uk/
Published by the Institute of Chartered Accountants in England and Wales.

Accountancy Age
http://www.accountancyage.com

British Medical Journal
http://www.bmj.com

Campaign
http://www.campaignlive.com
Magazine for the advertising industry.

Caterer & Hotelkeeper
http://www.caterer.com
Includes a vacancy listing.

Chemistry and Industry Magazine
http://ci.mond.org
This is a publication of the Society of the Chemical Industry, which contains a guide to job hunting on the internet for chemists.

Industry-specific contacts..

Address http://www.caterer.com/Jobs/index.htm   Go   Link

caterer.com

○ HOME   ○ CONTACT US   ○ SITE GUIDE   ○ ADVERTISING

Breaking News
Special Reports
Archive
Jobs
Web Links
Products
Directory
Events
Property

Jobs: Search

Your first stop for hospitality jobs in the UK and overseas.

Select the job function, location and type of organisation to search.
There are 4305 jobs available for searching.

Job Function
To make multiple selections hold down Ctrl key

All
Burser
Catering Director
Catering Manager
Catering Supervisor

Location
To make multiple selections hold down Ctrl key

All
Asia
East Anglia
East Midlands
Eire

SEARCH
RESET

Specialists in Hospitality
Recruitment...

Fig. 44. The web site of the magazine, *Caterer & Hotelkeeper*, is a valuable source of news and appointments throughout the hospitality industry.

Communications International
http://www.totaltele.com/cilive/
The telecommunications magazine from the publisher group EMAP.

Computing
http://www.computingnet.co.uk
The site includes a CV and interviews clinic.

Current Archaeology
http://www.compulink.co.uk/~archaeology/
The site includes career information for archaeologists, *The Directory of British Archaeology* and a listing of digs.

dotElectronics
http://www.dotelectronics.co.uk
A source of news, information and job vacancies in the field of electronics.

dotFarming
http://www.dotfarming.co.uk
This is a gateway to several farming magazines.

dotPharmacy
http://www.dotpharmacy.co.uk
The site contains highlights from *Chemist & Druggist* magazine.

Economist
http://www.economist.com
From the home page follow the link to Careers, where you will find classifieds and 'job postings for global executives'.

EFL Web
http://www.u-net.com/eflweb/
This is a professional magazine for teachers of English as a Foreign Language.

Electronic Telegraph
http://www.telegraph.co.uk
This is the *Telegraph*'s classified section online, but you have to register first.

ELT News
http://www.eltnews.com/
An online news sheet for English language teaching in Japan. It contains vacancies.

Environmental Data Services
http://www.ends.co.uk
EDS provides an environmental news service, a directory of environmental consultancies and a list of vacancies for environment professionals.

Estates Gazette Interactive
http://www.egi.co.uk
Estates Gazette is the leading weekly trade journal for the property industry. It contains regular job vacancies.

Financial Times
http://www.ft.com
The site maintains a substantial appointments section, but you must register first.

Guardian
http://www.guardian.co.uk
The newspaper contains a wide variety of jobs of interest to applicants interested in working in the public services. There are excellent search facilities, and you can receive notification by email of matching jobs.

Health Club Management
http://www.health-club.co.uk/healthclub/index.html
This official magazine of the Fitness Industry Association includes details of health and fitness jobs.

Health Service Journal
http://www.hsj.co.uk
The site typically contains several hundred healthcare management vacancies.

Housing Today
http://www.housingtoday.org.uk
The weekly magazine for social housing providers includes a jobs section.

Industry-specific contacts...

In Brief
http://www.inbrief.co.uk
This is a monthly legal magazine which contains a 'Bluffer's Guide to London Firms'.

Information for Industry
http://www.ifi.co.uk
The environmental publishing company has a business directory for the environment industry. You need to register (free).

Inside Housing
http://www.insidehousing.co.uk
They say: 'Search our dedicated database of 100 housing jobs and find a new job today.'

Language International
http://www.language-international.com
A magazine for language professionals.

Language Today
http://shop.logos.it/language_today/
An online magazine for everyone working in applied languages – translators, interpreters, terminologists, lexicographers and technical writers.

Law Society Gazette
http://www.lawgazette.co.uk
The journal of the Law Society of England and Wales, the professional body for solicitors.

Lawyer
http://www.the-lawyer.co.uk
Follow the top link to Lawyer Jobs. The site provides good national and international coverage. There is a law firm directory and recruitment consultant directory.

Leisure Marketing
http://www.leisuremedia.co.uk/Lopps/markwebsite.html

Leisure Opportunities Daily
http://www.leisuremedia.co.uk/Lopps/LOwebsite.html
The site includes current vacancies for people seeking work in the recreation, leisure and sports sectors.

LeisureWeek
http://www.leisureweek.co.uk
Check out *LeisureMoves*, a career magazine for the fitness and recreation market, complete with job vacancies.

Fig. 45. The leisure industry offers a great variety of possibilities. A visit to the web site of Leisure Jobs could be just the thing to get you started.

Marketing Online
http://www.marketing.haynet.com
Marketing Online is produced by *Marketing* magazine for client marketers and their agencies. Follow the link to Jobs.

Marketing Week
http://193.132.29.192/

Le Monde
http://www.lemonde.fr
This is the online version of the famous French newspaper. An English version is available. Look for job vacancies under 'L'espace emplois'. There are usually some UK vacancies.

Nature
http://www.nature.com
Nature is the leading international weekly journal of science. You can search for jobs, post your CV and check out career information.

New Scientist
http://www.newscientist.com
This site has recently been overhauled and you no longer need to register to use it or to see the many jobs available here. It claims to provide 'the most comprehensive listing of current science, technology and academic vacancies available on the web.' It is updated every Thursday.

Nursing Standard
http://www.nursing-standard.co.uk
Follow the link to jobs in nursing where there is a searchable database of nursing vacancies.

Industry-specific contacts..

People Management
http://www.peoplemanagement.co.uk
This is a magazine for the human resources sector. It contains job vacancies.

Pharmnews
http://pharmnews.com
Information for the pharmaceutical industry – includes vacancies.

PR Week
http://www.prweekuk.com
This is a service for people working in public relations. Use the pop-up menu and follow the link to Appointments.

Public Finance
http://www.cipfa.org.uk/PFO/
The site is maintained by the Chartered Institute of Public Finance and Accountancy.

Fig. 46. With opportunities in many of the top high street names, the Retail Careers web site is a must if you envisage a career in the distribution industry.

Retail Careers
http://www.retailcareers.co.uk
The site features a large selection of ever-changing vacancies from many of the UK's leading retailers and recruitment consultancies. Follow the link to Graduates, where you will find a salary survey, and tips on how to succeed in assessment tests.

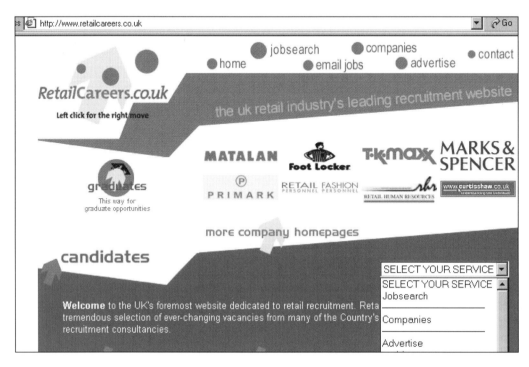

Science's Next Wave
http://www.nextwave.org
This is an online science careers magazine from *Science Online*.

Stage
http://www.thestage.co.uk
Stage is the leading periodical of the UK entertainment industry. The site has a good selection of links to theatre companies, theatres and other relevant organisations.

The Appointment Online
http://www.theappointment.co.uk/
This is a career magazine targeted at people working in the retail sector. Here, you'll find vacancies from retail management to personnel and training.

The Food Site
http://www.thefoodsite.com
This is a news magazine for the food industry. The jobs database typically contains around 250 vacancies.

Times Educational Supplement
http://www.tes.co.uk
The *TES* is the top weekly publication for teachers in primary, secondary and further education. It always contains a large number of vacancies.

Times Higher Education Supplement Internet Service
http://www.thesis.co.uk
THESIS offers a full range of academic jobs and research appointments. You can browse or search the database. The job ads go online on Tuesdays, and the news headlines and summaries on Fridays.

US Chronicle of Higher Education
http://chronicle.com
This is a publication relating to the US academic sector. It contains job vacancies.

Other useful contacts

Amazing Exotics Education Centre
http://www.amazingexotics.com
This is a sophisticated web site offering, among other things, an educational compound that provides training in the management, husbandry, performance and care of exotic animals.

Animal Care & Equine Training Organisation
http://www.horsecareers.co.uk
Through this site, you can access NVQs and SVQs, national traineeships, modern apprenticeships, interactive catalogue of all UK courses and colleges plus bulletin board and links.

PERFORMANCE
Actors
Cruise Work
Dancers
Entertainers
Musicians
Models
Vocalists

THEATRE WORLD
Backstage/Tech
Education
Front of House
Admin/Finance
Marketing/PR
Directing/Producir

Industry-specific contacts..

Applause Music Careers
http://www.cnvi.com/applause/
'Learn how to start an exciting career in the music and entertainment production touring industry! We cover it all, from performing and artist management to sound, light, and technical production.'

BPP
http://www.bppluton.co.uk
Through this site you can access fast-track courses leading to all the major accounting qualifications in the UK.

British Army
http://www.army.mod.uk/army/recruit/index2.htm
As Britain's largest employer, the Army has over 15,000 vacancies annually for people of all ages, abilities and educational standards.

CAPITB Trust
http://www.careers-in-clothing.co.uk
This is the national training organisation for the British clothing industry responsible for promoting careers, education, and vocational qualifications. You can find details here of their work and help if you are considering a career in the industry.

Careers in Law
http://www.cas.bris.ac.uk/careersin/law.htm
The Careers Advisory Service at the University of Bristol has produced this useful legal careers index.

CCETSW
http://www.ccetsw.org.uk
This site represents the main education and training body for social work.

Certify Now
http://www.certifynow.co.uk
This is a one-stop resource for certification information. Click onto UK training centre list, newsletters, courses, trainer's resources, downloads, CBT and study books. A vast information resource for those seeking professional computing qualifications.

CISC
http://www.cisc.org.uk
CISC is a forum for NVQs/SVQs at professional, managerial and technical levels in planning, construction, property and related engineering services. Click on the national occupational standards database, newsletter, contacts and events.

City & Finance Graduate Careers
http://www.gti.co.uk/city/
This is a site for graduates aspiring to accountancy and finance careers in the UK (Figure 47).

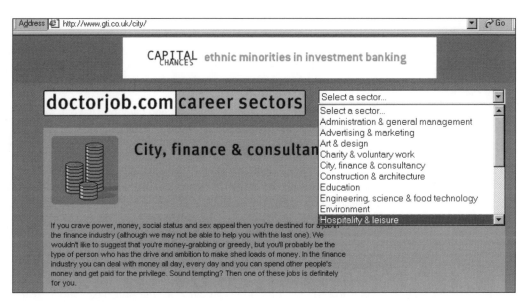

| Address | http://www.gti.co.uk/city/ |

CAPITAL CHANCES ethnic minorities in investment banking

doctorjob.com career sectors

Select a sector...

Select a sector...
Administration & general management
Advertising & marketing
Art & design
Charity & voluntary work
City, finance & consultancy
Construction & architecture
Education
Engineering, science & food technology
Environment
Hospitality & leisure

City, finance & consultan

If you crave power, money, social status and sex appeal then you're destined for a job in the finance industry (although we may not be able to help you with the last one). We wouldn't like to suggest that you're money-grabbing or greedy, but you'll probably be the type of person who has the drive and ambition to make shed loads of money. In the finance industry you can deal with money all day, every day and you can spend other people's money and get paid for the privilege. Sound tempting? Then one of these jobs is definitely for you.

Fig. 47. City & Finance Graduate Careers could be a good starting point if you see yourself as a potential City high flyer.

Community Work Resources
http://www.community-work-training.org.uk
The site is produced by the West Yorkshire Community Work Training Group and offers training material for community workers and other working in community based settings, material on anti-discriminatory practice and link to other useful sites.

Conference of Drama Schools
http://www.drama.ac.uk
This site links to member schools offering courses in theatre and media.

English Nursing Board
http://www.enb.org.uk
Visit this site for information on nursing and midwifery.

Environment Council
http://www.greenchannel.com/tec/doec/main.htm
This site gives the visitor a guide to academic, professional and vocational courses related to the environment. The online directory consists of a number of pages giving background information and advice to the potential students and a searchable database of UK environmental courses.

European Commission Representation in the UK
http://www.cec.org.uk
This site offers good access to lots of EC information plus a vacancy section.

Graduate Teacher Training Registry
http://www.gttr.ac.uk
This is a clearing house for PGCE applications. The site also includes a course vacancy list.

Industry-specific contacts...

HTML Writers Guild
http://www.hwg.org
The site includes online training courses.

Law Careers Advice Network
http://www.lcan.csu.ac.uk
This is the site of those involved in providing careers advice to law students and individuals considering a career in law.

Music Education Directory
http://www.bpi-med.co.uk/pages/bpi/index.html
Here, you will find instrumental and technical courses plus jobs in the music industry.

NISS
http://www.niss.ac.uk/cr/index.html#nb
NISS is a major internet gateway into higher education online in the UK. From this page you can access HE vacancies in administration, support and research.

Oxford Website for Library Trainees
http://www.lib.ox.ac.uk/owl/home.html
If you are thinking about information work this is the site for you.

National Examining Body for Supervision Management
http://www.nebsmgt.co.uk
Through this site, you can access information about the organisation that runs management training and development courses and workshops at more than 1,000 centres in the UK and Ireland.

Radio Frequency Engineering Education Initiative
http://www.rfeei.org.uk/rfeei.htm
Here you can find career profiles, links to companies and other useful sites.

RAF Careers
http://www.raf-careers.raf.mod.uk
Test your skills on a virtual mission to recover a stolen fighter plane. This is a high-tech guide to the many jobs offered by Britain's airborne fighting force. If you think you fit the bill you can apply online.

Royal Navy
http://www.royal-navy.mod.uk
Here you can find out what's new now, what happens next, what happened when, as well as careers information.

Social Science Research Grapevine
http://www.grapevine.bris.ac.uk
This site includes vacancies and training opportunities.

GRAPEVINE

What is Grapevine?

Conferences
Courses
Departments
CVs
Likeminds

8 Doing your own thing

In this chapter we will explore:

▶ *freelance and self-employment*
▶ *financial support*
▶ *telecommuting opportunities*

. . . .

In many ways, it has never been easier to start your own business enterprise. Communications are excellent, social change is throwing up opportunities everywhere, technology and information are readily available, and numerous support services can be accessed. But before you take the plunge consider:

▶ *The risks* – More hard work than you ever dreamed of, suffering relationships, financial crises, savage competitors, unexpected setbacks, possible isolation amid your problems, and a seemingly endless list of essential deadlines to meet and problems to be sorted.

▶ *The rewards* – Personal satisfaction and self-fulfilment, independence of mind, spirit and action, the respect and envy of others, and (if successful) more money in your pocket than you ever imagined.

Freelancing and self-employment

Ants
http://www.ants.com/ants/
This site offers to match freelancers with businesses who want to outsource projects which can be completed remotely.

Business Matters
http://www.business.knowledge.com
Here you can find information for people with new businesses, from starting-up to day-to-day issues.

Business Sales
http://www.businesssales.com
Through this site, you can find out about businesses for sale by owners and agents. You should seek the advice of a qualified accountant or lawyer if you are serious.

Consult Direct
http://www.kelwin.co.uk/ConsultDirect/about.htm
This is a directory of consultants, freelancers and contractors. Advertisers can present themselves with a company profile, a CV or a résumé.

Federation of Small Businesses
http://www.fsb.org.uk
The FSB protects, promotes, and furthers the interests of the self-

employed and small business sector throughout the United Kingdom. It might be worth joining for the practical and moral support you could obtain, including business networking.

Franchise Business
http://www.franchisebusiness.co.uk
This organisation offers a focal point for UK franchisers and franchisees.

Freelance BBS
http://www.freelancebbs.com/
The Freelance bulletin board service is designed to help freelancers and their prospective employers identify and get in touch with each other.

Freelance Informer
http://www.freelanceinformer.co.uk
Resources for the IT contracting sector can be found through this home page. Register to access job postings, news, information on recruiters and training, and advice for new contractors.

Freelance Marketplace
http://247malls.com/OS/cj/ants.htm
This is where you can find your marketplace community for independent contractors and freelance opportunities. Browse through the job listing to find freelance opportunities that match your interests including writing, marketing, translation, programming and design.

Freelance Online
http://www.freelanceonline.com
Through this US site, you can access jobs, message boards, a searchable directory of over 700 freelancers, frequently asked questions, resources, and networking opportunities for freelance professionals.

Freelance Solicitors Groups
http://members.aol.com/pjmiller00/freelance.html
The Freelance Solicitors Group represents the interests of those solicitors in England and Wales who work as solicitor for others on a locum, contract or freelance basis. Its activities include: a network of professional and social contacts, advice to members, making The Law Society aware of the interests of freelance solicitors and providing a list of prospective employers and entries in *The Law Society's Directory* of those members available for freelance, contract or locum work.

Freelancers
http://www.freelancers.net
The Freelancers Network maintains an open database of UK and global internet freelancers. It is free to be listed and free to search for freelancers. It gives you your own easy-to-remember web address which you can point to your own portfolio, CV or résumé.

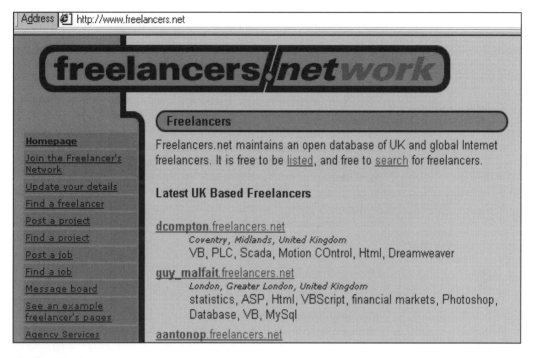

Fig. 48. The Freelancers Network is worth checking if you are considering the self-employment option.

Go Contract!
http://www.gocontract.com
This site helps would-be computer consultants set up in business.

Guru
http://www.guru.com
Guru is an established internet exchange in which independent professionals can connect with current or forthcoming contract projects.

HireAbility
http://www.hireability.com
This is a service company that provides a link between businesses needing specialised work performed and those with the ability to get the job done. It has freelancing, telecommuting, contract, consulting, writing, artistic, marketing, sales and other types of work available.

Hit Squad Freelancers
http://www.hitsquad.co.uk/free.htm
This site is aimed at the freelancer DTP professional. Whether you are a PC user or a Mac user, a visit to this site might bring you some work.

HomeRun
http://homerun.co.uk
Here, based on the entrepreneurial magazine of the same name, you can explore some UK resources for home workers and small businesses, which you can use to help start and run your business successfully.

Doing your own thing..

Jobsunlimited

http://www.jobsunlimited.co.uk

You can search for freelance work in *The Guardian* and its sister newspaper *The Observer* via this site.

Outsource 2000

http://outsource2000.com

OutSource2000 has joined forces with some of the leading sources in the home-based work related industry to create an online forum where individuals throughout the United States, Canada and the world can now receive continuously updated information relating to all aspects of working from home.

Ownbase

http://www.ownbase.com

OwnBase is an established business and social network. It has been providing a national business and social network since 1986. Membership is open to anyone who works from home (whether employed by an organisation or self-employed), as well as anyone interested in home working or the home-based economy. It publishes six newsletters a year, giving advice and information on business matters, advertising members' services, putting members in touch with each other and organising seminars on homeworking. OwnBase is a voluntary organisation, run by its members, for its members. They say: 'Getting actively involved means you'll get to know like-minded people who could become your clients or suppliers as well as your friends.'

Fig. 49. Ownbase is an established network for freelancers and the self-employed.

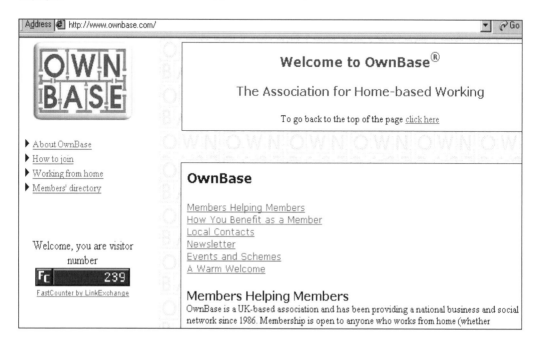

Shell LiveWire
http://www.shell-livewire.org
The mighty international oil company offers some sound advice to budding entrepreneurs aged 16 to 30 about how to set up and develop their own businesses. This great looking site has information about their Young Entrepreneur of the Year award scheme, and a discussion forum.

Smarterwork
http://www.smarterwork.com
Smarterwork says it is the complete virtual office. It can help you find the right people, a secure environment, and all the tools you need to work with others on projects. Its global payment system ensures that you really can do business with people all over the world. The freelance work involved includes writing, editing, graphic design, web build support, and document production.

Financial support

3i
http://www.3i.com
Quite a large number of venture capital companies have experience in putting up capital for internet start-up businesses. Backed and funded by major British financial institutions, the established firm of 3i ('Investors In Industry') is one of the biggest venture capital organisations in Europe, with enormous experience of helping small and medium sized enterprises to grow.

Best Grants Database in Britain
http://www.enterprise.net/cds/grants/
This one-page site offers details of a database of more than 300 grants available from the European Union, plus some 1,000 other grants available from the UK government. It also contains details of grants paid out by Training and Enterprise Councils, and local authorities. There is a separate grants database for Scotland.

British Venture Capital Association
http://www.bvca.co.uk
This association represents the top players in the venture capital industry. Its web site features various downloadable documents in PDF format including information about that informal source of venture capital, so-called business angels (private investors with cash to spare).

Community Research and Development Information Service
http://www.cordis.lu
CORDIS is an initiative of the European Union. It can help you to participate in EU-funded research programmes, find partners, and transfer your innovative ideas. The site is available in several languages.

Crescendo Ventures
http://www.crescendoventures.com/index_flat.html
This is the site of an international venture-capital organisation specialis-

ing in early-stage investment opportunities in the communications and ebusiness fields. It has bases in London, Minneapolis and Palo Alto, California.

EU Information Society Projects
http://www.ukishelp.co.uk
There are some excellent new opportunities for UK enterprises to obtain funding from the European Union (EU) for innovative development and application projects involving IT, multimedia, telecoms, broadcasting and electronic commerce.

Financial Aspects of Freelancing
http://www.brentwoodit.demon.co.uk/financia.htm
From here, you can order this free book which guides the computer free-lancer through the financial maze. Its authors are Barry Whiffin and Joanne Berry, accountants with over 25 years' experience of handling the taxation affairs of computer freelancers.

FIND Financial Directory
http://www.find.co.uk/businesses/
FIND is one of the established internet-based directories of UK financial services.

Four Leaf
http://www.fourleaf.com
Fourleaf aims to bring together internet startups, companies, investors and their professional advisers. DealBase – its online database of deals and dealmakers – allows you to look for the partners you need. You may be able to access capital, form strategic alliances, or locate business advice at various stages of your business growth.

Grant Aid
http://www.grantaid.com
Grant Aid is a commercial grant-finding service operating on a no-win, no-fee basis, linked to the Institute of Independent Business.

Loan Guarantee Scheme
http://www.dti.gov.uk/support/sflgs.htm
If you need help to obtain a bank loan for your business, the long-established loan guarantee scheme run by the Department of Trade & Industry may be the answer. It has helped thousands of small UK businesses over the years.

Start-It
http://www.start-it.co.uk/homepage/index.html
Here you can find out about a venture capital company with a specific interest in the IT and internet sectors and which offers financial, management and accounting support to start-ups.

Telecommuting opportunities

BT Working from Home
http://www.wfh.co.uk
Whether you are already working from home, or just thinking about it, this site should help you make the most of the liberating possibilities of telework. Here you'll find guidance and advice for setting up your home office, as well as resources that can help you from day to day.

European Telework Online
http://www.eto.org.uk
This is the internet portal for teleworking, telecommuting, and related topics. This telework and telecommuting portal site is linked to from more than 2,500 places on the internet world wide!

Flexibility
http://www.flexibility.co.uk/award.htm
Lots of telecommuting links are available through these pages. The telecommuting link will bring up a large number of links (mostly US).

TCA
http://www.tca.org.uk/home.htm
The TCA provides advice on how to approach teleworking, and information on the relevant technology. It offers examples of how other people progress – and uniquely – information about work opportunities. In the bi-monthly magazine, *Teleworker*, and in a weekly electronic bulletin the TCA sends out updates and information about full-time and temporary telework opportunities. You can join online.

Telecommuting Jobs
http://tjobs.com/
From the home page of this site, you can explore telecommuting with employers in the USA or anywhere else in the world. There are opportunities for artists, writers, web designers, data entry staff, desktop publishers, engineers, programmers, sales people and photographers. There are links to an online newsletter and other resources. View 60,000 telecommuting work from home job opportunities, enter your résumé,

Telelink Training for Europe
http://www.marble.ac.uk/telep/telework/tlpfolder/tlp.html
The TTE project is a European Community (Euroform) funded project which seeks to develop training opportunities in the field of teleworking. It has set up a network of telecottages and training centres around Europe designed to provide training support and service points for telework skills.

Teleweb
http://toucan-europe.co.uk/projects/teleweb/index.html
Teleweb aims to provide support on the web in a manner that is easy to understand and access. Although there is a fair amount of information

available about teleworking, there is a concern that teleworkers may not know where to obtain support. Teleweb aims to overcome these concerns by providing a one-stop location for this support.

Telework Training Resources
http://www.icbl.hw.ac.uk/telep/telework/ttrfolder/typfolder/typ.html
The directory section is designed to provide teleworkers with a directory for information on various telework organisations, associations, projects and services. It covers the UK and Europe.

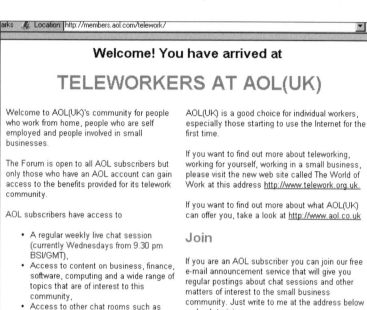

Teleworkers at AOL
http://members.aol.com/telework/
Run by the online service provider America Online, this is a community set up for people who work from home, people who are self employed, and people involved in running small businesses. The Forum is open to all AOL subscribers but only those who have an AOL account can gain access to the benefits provided for its telework community. If you want to find out more about teleworking, working for yourself, working in a small business, you can follow the link from here to a web site called The World of Work:

http://www.telework.org.uk.

Teleworkers Website
http://members.aol.com/telwebsite/index.htm
TWS provides a central location for UK teleworkers to announce their services and skills to prospective employers or clients for free. Any teleworker based in the UK can ask for their details to be placed on this site free of charge. You will be placed free of charge in an appropriate category decided by the services you offer.

Teleworking
http://www.netway.co.uk/users/teleworking.services/
This site provides information and services on teleworking, remote working, finding work and working from home.

Teleworking Web Directory
http://www.users.zetnet.co.uk/maac/myron/telework/twwdir.htm
You can find lots of teleworking links on this page.

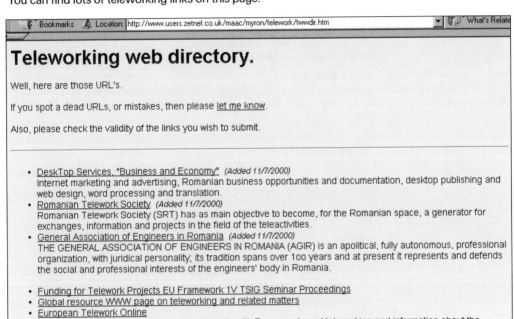

Telework Training Resources
http://www.icbl.hw.ac.uk/telep/telework/ttrfolder/typfolder/typ.html
This is designed to provide teleworkers with a directory of information
about various telework organisations, associations, projects and services. It covers both the UK and Europe.

More Internet Handbooks to help you

Personal Finance on the Internet, Graham Jones.
Marketing Your Business on the Internet, Sara Edlington (2nd edition).
Working from Home on the Internet, Laurel Alexander.

9 The best of the rest

In this chapter we will explore:

- ▶ *disabilities*
- ▶ *exhibitions and events*
- ▶ *graduate associations*
- ▶ *higher education links*
- ▶ *international opportunities*
- ▶ *learning about technology*
- ▶ *management training*
- ▶ *student support*
- ▶ *test and self assessments*
- ▶ *UK government information*
- ▶ *voluntary work for graduates*
- ▶ *work experience*

Disabilities

CanDo
http://cando.lancs.ac.uk
CanDo stands for the Careers Advisory Network on Disability Opportunities. It is the UK's official information service covering employment and careers issues for disabled students and graduates, and interested staff. Disabled HE students and graduates are offered information and advice on funding, rights, support services, disclosure, and work experience opportunities. There are details of the disability policies and practices in each of the UK's universities (known as Disability Statements). Disability organisations can use the site to promote their relevant services to disabled graduates in or seeking employment.

Disabled Graduates (AGCAS)
http://www.prospects.csu.man.ac.uk/student/cidd/links/Disabled.htm
This is a page of links maintained by the Association of Graduate Careers Advisory Services (AGCAS).

Disability Net
http://www.disabilitynet.co.uk/info/education/index.html
From the home page, you can access national and international links to education and training and archive material.

Dorton Training Services (Royal London Society for the Blind)
http://www.rlsb.or.uk/reader/dts.html
There are 10 links on this simple web site: training opportunities, employment skills, technology centre, partnerships, enrolment, testimonials and

contacts. DTS offers RSA NVQs, City & Guilds qualifications, ESOL, Braille reading and writing skills, IT skills, and mobility and orientation skills.

Karten CTEC Centre
http://www.ctec.org.uk/index.html
A registered charity, Karten is one of the UK's leading suppliers of computer-aided training and education for disabled people, people with special needs and people with learning disabilities. Other services include training in using computers and associated specialist hardware and software for teachers working with disabled people, carers of the disabled, advocates of disabled people and relatives of the disabled.

Exhibitions and events

AIESEC
http://www.uk.aiesec.org
AIESEC is the world's largest international, student-run organiser of international graduate exchanges and careers fairs. Represented in more than 80 countries, it has a membership of more than 50,000 people, including on 23 campuses in the UK. Its primary focus is on the exchange of graduates and undergraduates between various countries in the fields of business, management, finance, marketing, engineering and economics.

EMDS
http://www.emdsnet.com
Geared very much to the global recruitment market, EMDS organises a number of job fairs each year. These include Euro Managers, Asia Managers Forum, and Africa Managers Forum. Its expertise lies in connecting

Fig. 50. EMDS can keep you up to date about forthcoming recruitment fairs and events.

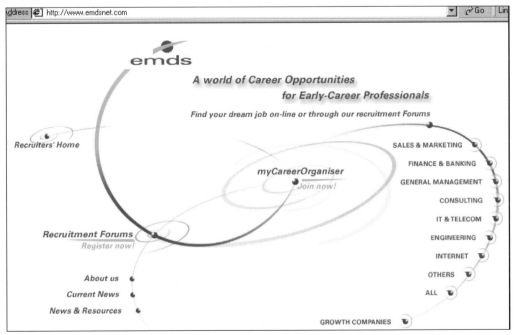

high-calibre graduates and early-career professionals from all parts of the globe with the world's leading employers. The company itself currently has 250 administrative staff in 21 offices in 17 countries.

National Graduate Recruitment Exhibitions
http://www.gradjobs.co.uk
This is a useful guide to the regular graduate recruitment fairs held at Birmingham University and the National Exhibition Centre, and supported by The Guardian newspaper and other sponsors.

Personal Development Show
http://www.personalshow.co.uk
The Personal Development Show is one of the leading events in the training and personal development calendar. The show is divided into zones: the home office, careers and learning, recruitment and lifestyle.

Visit
http://www.visit.haynet.com
Haymarket hosts the UK's largest systems and IT recruitment events held in London, Manchester and other cities.

Graduate associations and networks

Association of MBAs
http://www.mba.org.uk
The UK-based Association of MBAs is a global network dedicated to raising public, business, and academic awareness of the MBA. It promotes improvement in management standards and offers advice and information. You can use the site to search for an MBA programme to suit you.

National Association of Graduate-Professional Students (US)
http://www.nagps.org/NAGPS/
Through its national office and regional networks, NAGPS acts as a clearinghouse for information on graduate and professional student groups at all stages of development.

National Postgraduate Committee
http://www.npc.org.uk
The NPC is a representative body for postgraduates in the UK. It is made up of student representatives from educational institutions with postgraduate students. The NPC aims to promote the interests of postgraduates studying in the UK, while remaining politically non-aligned. It holds an annual conference, and publishes various guidelines and codes of practice. Its links page can connect you to the web pages of various postgraduate associations and societies across the UK.

Political Studies Association Graduate Network
http://www.psa.ac.uk/graduate/default.htm
The Graduate Network represents the interests of postgraduate students within the PSA, maintains links between postgraduate students through-

out the UK, and helps to integrate postgraduates into the wider academic community.

Social Sciences Grapevine
http://www.sosig.ac.uk/gv/
Grapevine is a source of research, training and development opportunities in the social sciences. You can explore research profiles of like-minded people, put your CV online and search for others.

UK Student Unions Index
http://www.stu.uea.ac.uk/info/uksu.html
Run from the University of East Anglia, this claims to be the most comprehensive list of UK student unions. It is kept up to date with help from the unions themselves.

University of Bristol Graduate Association
http://www.bris.ac.uk/Depts/GradAssoc/

Higher education links

BBC Learning Zone – Open University
http://www.bbc.co.uk/education/lzone/gen.shtml
This site offers a variety of support and links. You can check out the BBC's full range of educational programmes in special subject pages ranging from Art and Design to Social Studies and Technology.

Euro Study Centres
http://bridge.anglia.ac.uk/www/eurostudy.html
The Euro Study Centre network has centres providing information and services about higher education courses available through flexible learning packages.

Listing of all HE Institutions
http://www.hesa.ac.uk/links/he_inst.htm
Here you will find one page listing all universities with their addresses, central phone numbers, fax numbers, chief officers and direct links. You can search by clicking on an alphabetical letter and then scrolling down. The site is maintained by HESA.

Ortelius
http://ortelius.unifi.it/ortelius/index2.html
This site offers a database on higher education in Europe. From the home page click on to institutes and courses (you need to subscribe to get into this one), institutional contracts, EU programmes, description of the national higher education systems, EU acts on higher education and subscription.

Peterson's Education
http://petersons.com
This substantial site contains details of over 7,500 US institutions of higher education offering post secondary awards, certificates, or diplo-

mas requiring less than the two years of study necessary for an associate degree. The programs at these schools are career oriented and their programs are primarily in the fields of business: real estate, banking, accounting, technology, personal services, health care and trade. However, many are in more academically based areas such as chemistry, library science, English composition and foreign language translation. Links include a bookstore and special schools, distance learning and contact points.

UCAS
http://www.ucas.co.uk
This site represents the Universities and Colleges Admissions Service for the UK, which processes applications for full-time undergraduate courses, Higher National Diplomas and university diplomas. The site includes general information about getting into a college or university.

UK Academic Sites
http://src.doc.ic.ac.uk/uk-academic.html
This site links to an enormous range of UK universities and other academic sites, giving links into their various departments. The opening page lists institutions in alphabetical order. Each link is maintained by the institution and offers course information including research and administration procedures. Some example links are the Open University, University of Brighton and the Political Studies Association.

UK Further Education Higher Education & University Colleges
http://www.bham.ac.uk/webmaster/ukuwww.html
Produced by the University of Birmingham, this site offers links to UK further and higher educational web sites. They are listed in alphabetical order or you can click on to an alphabetical letter. When you access the institute of your choice, you can then access their web site. There are also references to other web sites where you can search for information on further and higher education institutions.

UK Sensitive Maps
http://scitsc.wlv.ac.uk/ukinfo/uk.map.html
This site is produced by the University of Wolverhampton and offers access to higher education institutes. You can access institutional web sites via the map on the home page. By clicking onto the options on the left-hand side of the home page, you can access specific information related to the institute such as prospectuses for undergraduates and postgraduates, research, the library and links.

UK Universities and Further Education Colleges
http://www.ja.net/janet-sites/university.html
The UK Academic & Research Network or JANET offers a brief home page with the letters of the alphabet waiting for you to click on to them to access institution web sites. There are three icons on the home page. One leads you to JANET telling you that JANET connects several hundred institutions, including universities and colleges plus research council

establishments and other organisations that work in collaboration with the academic and research community. There are icons for help and sites, which offers links to other organisations that have JANET connections.

▶ See also – *Education & Training on the Internet*, Laurel Alexander (Internet Handbooks).

International opportunities

American Work Experience
http://www.awe-recruitment.freeserve.co.uk
AWE recruits European staff to work for about nine weeks in US children's summer camps. Applicants should be aged 18 to 31 and meet certain clearly stated criteria.

British Universities North America Club
http://www.bunac.org
BUNAC is a non-profit, non-political student organisation with its own travel company. Formed in 1962 by students from North America Clubs and Canada Clubs at universities throughout the UK, BUNAC continues to be represented on British campuses by enthusiastic ex-participants. One of BUNACamp's founders, John Ball, began taking groups of camp counsellors to North America as long ago as 1953. Today, the organisation makes it possible for young people, all over the world, to participate in similar programmes worldwide.

Fig. 51. The British Universities North America Club (BUNAC). Having started with summer camps in the USA, BUNACamp now offers work opportunities in many different countries.

143

The best of the rest ....

Our Magazine -
Overseas Jobs -
Moving Overseas -
Living Overseas -
Overseas Retirement
Unique Lifestyles -
Embassies -
Overseas Education -
Articles -
Classified Section -
COUNTRY

Escape Artist
http://www.escapeartist.com
If you are looking for a career overseas or want to be an internationally mobile professional anywhere, this huge site (4,000 pages plus) can provide links to everything you need to know. There are links to the world's newspapers, books, the world's search engines, a countries index, internet commerce, global investments, tax havens, stock markets, offshore real estate and banks, overseas jobs, embassies and more.

Eurograduate Live
http://www.eurograduate.com
This web site provides information about graduate opportunities across Europe. Tell them where you want to go, what type of work you want to do, and what your degree is in, and away you go. There is also guidance on careers abroad and details of opportunities for postgraduates.

Expat Network
http://www.expatnetwork.co.uk
If you are considering an international career move, this site will help you find a job overseas and back you up with ongoing support. Link into *Nexus,* a monthly magazine packed with expertly written articles.

First Point International
http://www.firstpointinter.com
First Point is a worldwide relocation specialist.

How to Get an Overseas Job
http://homepages.tesco.net/ ~ Ken.Creffield/
Fed up with the rat race? Got a year out and don't know what to do with it? This site supplies a wide range of job suggestions around the world and tells you where to look and who to approach to do something about it.

InternAbroad
http://www.internabroad.com
InternAbroad is a comprehensive online source for international internships, study abroad, jobs abroad, volunteer positions abroad, teaching positions abroad and a whole lot more.

International Medical Graduates on the World Wide Web
http://home.earthlink.net/ ~ alexfeo/
This is an excellent point of contact for medical graduates worldwide.

National Association of Managers of Student Services
http://www.namss.org.uk/study_other.htm
Here you will find a really excellent general-purpose collection of links. They cover applying to and studying in Europe, the United States and other countries around the world.

Naukri (India)
http://www.naukri.com
Naukri maintains links to placement agencies, major employers, career resources and advice. The site has a massive 13,000 company and other listings and 50,000 job vacancies, plus more than 7 million page views per month.

Network Overseas
http://www.networkoverseas.cc
Network Overseas recruits highly qualified professionals for posts in engineering and construction, information technology, teaching, medicine, nursing and ancillary hospital services for clients across the world. It has a special emphasis on the Middle East.

Overseas Jobs Express
http://www.overseasjobsexpress.co.uk
This web site offers a database of international vacancies. There is a guide to over 700 career, employment, job and recruiter sites throughout the world which you can access.

Fig. 52. The web site of the popular newspaper *Overseas Jobs Express*, an established source of vacancies and news for would-be expats.

The best of the rest ....

Teaching Abroad
http://www.teaching-abroad.co.uk
They say: 'Whether you teach with us in an Indian school or work with us on a conservation project in Mexico, whether you help with English classes in Moscow or do a veterinary project in Ghana, you will be in demand. Programmes are eye-opening and life-changing, and also enjoyable and sensibly planned.'

WelcomeIndia
http://www.welcomeindia.com/jobs/
This site offers extensive information and links on working in the US, Canada, Australia and New Zealand, as well as in the UK. You can also click onto seasonal and temporary work, careers information and contract work.

Yahoo! Countries
http://www.yahoo.co.uk/regional/countries/
Each country has a section on business and economy where you can find trade links, business opportunities, economic links, tax information, company listings and much more. This site makes a great starting point for your research.

▶ See also – *Overseas Job Hunting on the Internet*, Laurel Alexander (Internet Handbooks).

Learning about technology

BBC Education: Webwise
http://www.bbc.co.uk/education/webwise/
You will find over 1,000 pages of help, advice and jargon-busting news on what you need to get the best out of the net, whatever your level of experience.

Cyber Learning Centre
http://www.usa2100.org
This is a project of the National Education Foundation and Northern Virginia Community College. You can enrol in a Microsoft Certified Systems Engineer Scholarship Program. Applicants must have a college degree and/or operating systems experience and an interest in networking. On the site you can browse through a catalogue of over two hundred computer based training (CBT) products in the latest IT areas.

Individual Software
http://www.individualsoftware.com/corporate/cbtproducts.htm
Individual Software's computer-based software tutorials are interactive, self-paced training programs designed to help the novice, intermediate, and experienced user to get the most out of their PC and PC applications. The courses on offer include Windows, DOS and Macintosh.

Microsoft Training & Certifications
http://microsoft.com/train_cert/
Find out about training and certification courses link into courses, exams and training providers. Additional icons link to what's new, books, newsletters, curriculum and international sites.

National Computing Centre
http://www.ncceducation.co.uk
The NCC was formed by the UK government in 1966, to stimulate the growth of computer usage through the provision of information, guidance and training Today, NCC Education Services is one of the world's top independent IT training organisations. It supports over 400 training organisations in 30 countries, with some 25,000 students world wide receiving its qualifications each year.

Management training

Association of Business Schools
http://www.the-abs.org.uk
The ABS represents about 100 of the leading business schools of UK universities, higher education institutions and independent management colleges. It aims to promote the study of business and management to help improve the quality and effectiveness of managers in the UK and internationally. The site includes an online directory of UK business and management education.

Kogan Page Resources
http://www.kogan-page.co.uk
Kogan Page is a leading London-based publisher of books and materials for business managers. From its home page you can link to resources for career development, training and business management.

Management Training and Development Institute
http://www.mtdi.com
MTDI is a training, consulting, and research group. It focuses on assisting organisations in improving their quality, productivity, and creativity through the application of leading management theory and practices. MTDI offers training, consulting, assessment, and research services to businesses and government agencies in the US and other countries. It also conducts development programs that support public and private sector technology transfer initiatives worldwide.

Third Sector Project – Enablement Training for Global Non Profit Sector
http://www.jhu.edu/~ips/Programs/ThirdSectorProject/our.htm
This project is run by the John Hopkins University, USA. It gears the training of non-profit managers to the ethos and philosophy of the non-profit sector, combining professional managerial capability with a commitment to the empowerment of organisations, communities, and individuals. The programme is delivered through short-term internships, training workshops and training-the-trainer programs.

The best of the rest ....

▶ See also – *Managing the Internet in Your Organisation*, Ian Hosker (Internet Handbooks).

Student support

National Association of Managers of Student Services
http://www.namss.org.uk/banks_grad.htm
With its hundreds of intelligently organised links, the NAMSS web site is an essential bookmark for all students.

StudentsUK
http://www.studentuk.com
From the home page you can click on news, films, advice, a student soap, travel, music, careers, politics and sport. There is a search button on the home page. You can register to join UniverCity to chat. From the home page you can send ecards, take part in an opinion poll and go online shopping for gear and gigs. Another click will take you to GraduBase, a searchable database of graduate employers.

UK Socrates-Erasmus
http://speke.ukc.ac.uk/erasmus/erasmus/
From the home page, you can access information for students and universities about foreign study opportunities offered by the organisation in European countries, including answers to FAQs and regular newsletters.

Tests and self assessments

ASE
http://www.ase-solutions.co.uk/html/business/products/gmaex1.htm
This site offers some useful practice aptitude tests.

Brain
http://www.brain.com/
Try your hand at these free online tests on intelligence, mental performance, memory, emotional state and more. They could stand you in good stead when you starting talking to a prospective employer.

Civil Service Fast Stream
http://www.cabinet-office.gov.uk/civilservice-recruitment/1999/fast-stream/sap.htm
Try out the self-assessment programme on this site.

Fleming Banfu International
http://www.banfu.com
The services of this company include search, selection, psychometric assessment, and function profiling.

Keirsey Temperament Sorter & Temperament Theory
http://keirsey.com/
From this site you can explore Professor Keirsey's tests. Sometimes the test does not accurately identify your personality, but it may give you a

place to start looking for a portrait that fits. Perhaps after you have read many of the portraits, and even asked others which of the portraits best describe you, you may be able to begin to define your own personality.

SHL Direct
http://www.shlgroup.com
You can try out some practice aptitude tests here.

SIMA
http://www.sima.co.uk
SIMA stands for System for Identifying Motivated Abilities. It is a motivational process developed in America in the 1950s. It is used by this Oxford management consultancy to help executives discover 'what makes them tick'.

UK government information

DTI: Minimum Wage Regulations (UK)
http://www.dti.gov.uk/IR/nmw/
This is part of the web site of the Department of Trade & Industry (UK). It gives details of the minimum wage, with links to government legislation and other employment-related web sites.

DTI Regulatory Guides: Employment
http://www.dti.gov.uk/IR/regs.htm
Here you can find official fact sheets covering everything from disability discrimination to itemised pay statements.

Institute for Employment Research
http://www.warwick.ac.uk/ier/
The Institute for Employment Research is one of Europe's leading centres for research in the labour market field. Its work focuses upon the operation of labour markets and socio-economic processes related to employment and unemployment in the UK at national, regional and local levels. It includes comparative European research on employment and training.

Labour Research Department
http://www.lrd.org.uk/index.html
Visit this sit for press releases and offline publications on workplace issues such as equal opportunities and privatisation. The site is directed at employees.

Times Higher Educational Supplement Internet Service
http://www.timeshigher.newsint.co.uk
This THES site offers home and international news and vacancies in the post-compulsory education and research world. This online version apparently already achieves more 'hits' every day than the circulation of its long-standing print edition.

The best of the rest ....

University for Industry
http://national.learning.net.uk
This links to the UK government's project for a new University for Industry.

Working Benefits
http://www.workingbenefits.dss.gov.uk
The Department of Social Security presents a guide to state benefits for working people to encourage unemployed people back into work and tell people on low pay about benefits they can claim. You can find out about Family Credit, the Disability Working Allowance, the Back to Work Bonus, and other schemes.

Voluntary work for graduates

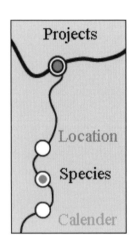

Ecovolunteer
http://www.ecovolunteer.org

Friends of the Earth
http://www.foe.co.uk
The Friends of the Earth Trust is an environmental charity which commissions detailed research and provides extensive information and educational materials. It is represented in 58 countries.

Frontier
http://www.frontierprojects.ac.uk
Explore the latest news on some worthwhile conservation projects in Africa and the Far East.

International Development
http://www.sussex.ac.uk/Units/CDU/cideve.html
This is a page of links gathered by the Sussex University Careers Development Unit.

One World
http://www.oneworld.org
Jobs and volunteer work in development and global justice organisations are offered through this web site.

Oxfam
http://www.oxfam.org.uk
The site includes details of job opportunities with Oxfam GB. You can search Oxfam's latest vacancies by job type or view all the current vacancies together.

Students Partnership Worldwide
http://www.spw.org
This is a development charity that sends graduates on educational and environmental programmes in Africa and Asia for five months.

VOIS
http://www.vois.org.uk
This site hosts a number of charity and voluntary organisations sites. You can browse by sector, by A-Z listing or by keyword.

Voluntary Service Overseas
http://www.vso.org.uk
VSO is one of the largest international operators in the voluntary work area.

Voluntary Work Online
http://www.voluntarywork.org.uk
Explore a database of hundreds of voluntary work and community service vacancies.

Work experience

British Journal of Work Experience
http://www.ncwe.com/UCEreport.html
This report considers the impact of sandwich education on the activities of graduates six months post-graduation.

Work Experience Bank
http://www.workbank.man.ac.uk
This is a resource for students, employers and academics. Using this site will give you access to information and work experience opportunities in the UK and overseas.

More Internet Handbooks to help you

Where to Find It on the Internet, Kye Valongo (2nd edition).

Visit the free Internet HelpZone at
www.internet-handbooks.co.uk
Helping you master the internet

Further reading

Beyond the CV, Helen Vandevelde (Butterworth Heinemann).

British Vocational Qualifications (Kogan Page). A directory of vocational qualifications available from all the awarding bodies in Britain.

Build Your Own Rainbow (Barrie Hopson & Mike Scally).

Career Networking, Laurel Alexander (How To Books).

Creating You & Co, William Bridges (Nicholas Brealey).

Directory of Jobs & Careers Abroad, Alex Lipinski (Vacation Work).

Education and Training on the Internet, Laurel Alexander (Internet Handbooks).

Finding a Job on the Internet, Brendan Murphy (Internet Handbooks, 2nd edition).

Get a Job Abroad, Roger Jones (How To Books).

Guide to Working Abroad, Godfrey Golzen (Daily Telegraph/Kogan Page).

Handbook of Free Careers Information (Trotman).

How to Pass Graduate Recruitment Tests (Kogan Page).

How to Succeed in Psychometric Tests (Sheldon Business Books).

Kelly's Business Directory. Contains information on more than 82,000 industrial, commercial and professional organisations in the UK.

Net That Job!, Irene Krechowiecka (Kogan Page).

Overseas Job Hunting on the Internet, Laurel Alexander (Internet Handbooks).

Strike a New Career Deal, Carole Pemberton (Pitman Publishing).

Teleworking Handbook (TCA).

Times 1000 List of Companies. Contains background information on major companies and establishments offering management and other training courses.

What Colour is Your Parachute (Richard Nelson Bolles).

Who Owns Whom. A directory of parent companies, their subsidiaries and associates.

Working from Home on the Internet, Laurel Alexander (Internet Handbooks).

Glossary of internet terms

access provider – The company that provides you with access to the internet. See also **internet service provider**.

ActiveX – A Microsoft programming language that allows effects such as animations, games and other interactive features to be included a web page.

Adobe Acrobat – A type of software required for reading PDF files ('portable document format').

address book – A directory in a web browser where you can store people's email addresses.

ADSL – Asymmetric Digital Subscriber Line, phone line technology designed to provide a much fast internet connection speed.

AOL – America OnLine, the world's biggest internet service provider, with some 27 million subscribers.

Apple Macintosh – A type of computer that has its own proprietary operating system, as distinct from the MSDOS and Windows operating systems found on PCs (personal computers).

applet – An application programmed in Java that is designed to run only on a web browser.

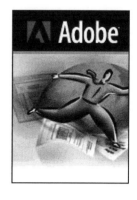

application – Any program, such as a word processor or spreadsheet program, designed for use on your computer.

ARPANET – Advanced Research Projects Agency Network, an early form of the internet.

ASCII – American Standard Code for Information Interchange. It is a simple text file format that can be accessed by most word processors and text editors.

attachment – A file sent with an email message.

bandwidth – The width of the electronic highway that gives you access to the internet. The higher the bandwidth, the wider this highway, and the faster the traffic can flow.

baud rate – The data transmission speed in a modem, measured in kps (kilobits per second).

BBS – Bulletin board service. A facility to read and to post public messages on a particular web site.

Blue Ribbon Campaign – An internet free speech campaign. See: http://www.eff.org

bookmarks – A file of URLs of your favourite internet sites. In the Internet Explorer browser and AOL they are called Favorites.

boolean search – A search in which you type in words such as AND and OR to refine your search. Such words are called 'Boolean operators'.

bot – Short for robot. It is used to refer to a program that will perform a task on the internet, such as carrying out a search.

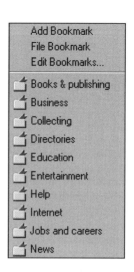

browser – Your browser is the program that you use to access the world wide web, and manage your personal communications and privacy when online. By far the two most popular browsers are Netscape Navigator and its dominant rival Microsoft Internet Explorer.

bug – A weakness in a program or a computer system.

bulletin board – A type of computer-based news service that provides an email service and a file archive.

cache – A file storage area on a computer. Your web browser will normally cache (copy to your hard drive) each web page you visit.

certificate – A computer file that securely identifies a person or organisation on the internet.

channel (chat) – Place where you can chat with other internet chatters. The name of a chat channel is prefixed with a hash mark, #.

Glossary of internet terms ....

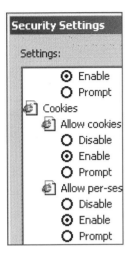

Dial-Up
Networking

client – This is the term given to the program that you use to access the internet. For example your web browser is a web client, and your email program is an email client.

configure – To set up, or adjust the settings, of a computer or software program.

content – The text, articles, images, columns and sales messages of a web site.

cookie – A cookie is a small text code that the server of a web page asks your browser to store on your hard drive. It may be used to store password or registration details, and pass information about your site usage to the web site concerned.

cracker – Someone who breaks into computer systems.

crash – What happens when a computer program malfunctions.

cyberspace – Popular term for the intangible 'place' where you go to surf – the ethereal world of computers and telecommunications on the internet.

data – Information. Data can exist in many forms such as numbers in a spreadsheet, text in a document, or as binary numbers stored in a computer's memory.

database – A store of information in digital form. Many web sites make use of substantial databases to deliver maximum content at high speed to the web user.

dial up account – This allows you to connect your computer to your internet provider's computer remotely.

digital – Based on the two binary digits, 1 and 0. The operation of all computers is based on this amazingly simple concept. All forms of information are capable of being digitised – numbers, words, and even sounds and images – and then transmitted over the internet.

directory – On a PC, a folder containing your files.

DNS – Domain name server.

domain name – A name that identifies an IP address. It identifies to the computers on the rest of the internet where to access particular information. Each domain has a name. For someone@somewhere.co.uk, 'somewhere.co.uk' is the domain name.

download – To copy a file from one computer on the internet to your own computer.

ebusiness – The broad concept of doing business to business, and business to consumer sales, over the internet.

ecash – Short for electronic cash.

ecommerce – The various means and techniques of transacting business online.

email – Electronic mail, any message or file you send from your computer to another computer using your 'email client' program (such as Netscape Messenger or Microsoft Outlook).

email address – The unique address given to you by your ISP. It can be used by others using the internet to send email messages to you.

emoticons – Popular symbols used to express emotions in email, for example the well known smiley :-) which means 'I'm smiling!' Emoticons are not normally appropriate for business communications.

encryption – The scrambling of information to make it unreadable without a key or password.

ezines – The term for magazines and newsletters published on the internet.

FAQs – Frequently asked questions.

Favorites – The rather coy term for **bookmarks** used by Internet Explorer, and by America Online.

file – Any body of data such as a word-processed document, a spreadsheet, a database file, a graphics or video file, sound file, or computer program.

filtering software – Software loaded onto a computer to prevent access to unwelcome content on the internet.

firewall – A firewall is special security software designed to stop the flow of certain files into and out of a computer network.

flame – A more or less hostile or aggressive message posted in a newsgroup or to an individual newsgroup user.

folder – The name for a directory on a computer. It is a place in which files are stored.

form – A web page that allows or requires you to enter information into fields on the page and send the information to a web site, program or individual on the web.

forums – Places for discussion on the internet. They include Usenet newsgroups, mailing lists, and bulletin board services.

frames – A web design feature in which web pages are divided into several areas or panels, each containing separate information.

freespace – An allocation of free web space by an internet service provider or other organisation.

freeware – Software programs made available without charge. Where a small charge is requested, the term is **shareware**.

FTP – File transfer protocol, the method the internet uses to speed files back and forth between computers.

GIF – Graphic interchange format. It is a widely-used compressed file format used on web pages and elsewhere to display files that contain graphic images. See also **JPEG** and **PDF**.

hacker – A person interested in computer programming, operating systems, the internet and computer security. In common usage, the term is often wrongly used to describe crackers.

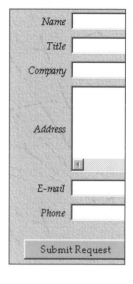

History list – A record of visited web pages, stored by your browser.

hits – The number of times that items on a web page have been viewed.

home page – The index or main page of a web site.

host – A host is the computer where a particular file or domain is located, and from where people can retrieve it.

HTML – Hyper text markup language, the universal computer language used to create pages on the world wide web.

HTTP – Hypertext transfer protocol, the protocol used by the world wide web.

hyperlink – See **link**.

hypertext – This is a link on an HTML page that, when clicked with a mouse, results in a further HTML page or graphic being loaded into view on your browser.

ICQ – A form of internet chat, derived from the phrase 'I seek you'.

internet – A broad term that encompasses email, web pages, internet chat, newsgroups, mailing lists, bulletin boards, and – video conferencing.

internet2 – A new form of the internet being developed exclusively for educational and academic use.

internet directory – A special web site which consists of categorised information about other web sites. The most widely used is Yahoo! at: http://www.yahoo.com

Internet Explorer – The world's most popular browser software, a product of Microsoft.

Internet protocol number – The numerical code that is a domain name's real address.

internet service providers – Organisations which offer people ('users') access to the internet. The well-known commercial ones in the UK include AOL, CompuServe, BT Internet, Freeserve, Demon and Virgin Net. Services typically include access to the world wide web, email and newsgroups, as well as others such as news, chat, and entertainment.

intranet – Software that uses internet technology to allow communication be-

Glossary of internet terms ....

tween individuals, for example within a large commercial organisation. It often operates on a LAN (local area network).

IP address – An 'internet protocol' address. All computers linked to the internet have one. The address is somewhat like a telephone number, and consists of four sets of numbers separated by dots.

IRC – Internet relay chat. The chat involves typing messages which are sent and read in real time

ISDN – Integrated services digital network, a high-speed telephone network for internet use.

JPEG or **JPG** – The acronym is short for Joint Photographic Experts Group. A JPEG is a specialised file format used to display graphic files on the internet.

kick – To eject someone from a chat channel.

LAN – A local area network, a computer network usually located in one building or campus.

link – A hypertext phrase or image that calls up another web page when you click on it.

LINX – The London Internet Exchange, the facility which maintains UK internet traffic in the UK.

listserver – An automated email system whereby subscribers are able to receive and send email from other subscribers to the list.

lurk – The slang term used to describe reading a newsgroup's messages without actually taking part in that newsgroup. Despite the connotations of the word, it is a perfectly respectable activity on the internet.

macros – 'Macro languages' are used to automate repetitive tasks in Word processors and other applications.

mail server – A remote computer that enables you to send and receive emails.

mailing list – A forum where messages are distributed by email to the members of the forum.

metasearch engine – A site that sends a keyword search to many different search engines and directories so you can use many search engines from one place.

modem – An internal or external piece of hardware plugged into your PC. It links into a standard phone socket, thereby giving you access to the internet. The word derives from MOdulator/DEModulator.

moderator – A person in charge of a mailing list, newsgroup or forum.

MPEG or **MPG** – The file format used for video clips available on the internet. See also JPEG. See http://mpeg.org for further technical information

MP3 – An immensely popular audio format that allows you to download and play music on your computer.

navigate – To click on the hyperlinks on a web site in order to move to other web pages or internet sites.

net – A slang term for the internet. In the same way, the world wide web is often just called the web.

netiquette – Popular term for the unofficial rules and language people follow to keep electronic communication in an acceptably polite form.

Netscape – After Microsoft's Internet Explorer, Netscape Navigator is the most popular browser software for surfing the internet.

newsgroup – A Usenet discussion group. There are 80,000 of them.

newsreader – A type of software that enables you to search, read, post and manage messages in a newsgroup. The best known are Microsoft Outlook, and Netscape Messenger.

news server – A remote computer (e.g. your internet service provider) that enables you to access newsgroups.

nick – Nickname, an alias you can give yourself and use when entering a chat channel, rather than using your real name.

OS – The operating system in a computer, for example MS DOS (Microsoft Disk Operating System), or Windows 95/98.

patch – A small piece of software used to patch up ('fix') a hole or defect ('bug') in a software program.

PC – Personal computer, based on IBM technology. It is distinct from the Apple Macintosh which uses a different operating system

PDA – Personal data assistant – a mobile phone, palm top or any other hand-held processor, typically used to access the internet.

PDF – Portable document format, a handy type of file produced using Adobe Acrobat software. It has universal applications for text and graphics.

PGP – Pretty Good Privacy, a proprietary and highly secure method of encoding a message before transmitting it over the internet.

plug in – A type of (usually free and downloadable) software required to add some form of functionality to web page viewing.

PoP – Point of presence. This refers to the dial-up phone numbers available from your ISP.

portal site – Portal means gateway. It is a web site designed to serve as a general jumping off point into the internet or to some particular part of it.

privacy – To explore internet privacy issues worldwide visit the Electronic Frontier Foundation at www.eff.org, and for the UK, www.netfreedom.org

protocol – Technical term for the method by which computers communicate.

proxy – An intermediate computer or server, used for reasons of security.

Quicktime – A popular free software program from Apple Computers. It is designed to play sounds and images including video clips and animations on both Apple Macs and personal computers.

radio button – A button that, when clicked, looks like this: ⊙

refresh, reload – The refresh or reload button on your browser toolbar tells the web page you are looking at to reload.

register – You may have to give your name, personal details and financial information to some sites before you can continue to use the pages.

router – A machine that direct internet data (network packets) from one internet location to another.

script – A script is a set of commands written into the HTML tags of a web page.

scroll, scroll bar – To scroll means to move part of a page or document into view or out of view on the screen. Scrolling is done by using a scroll bar activated by the mouse pointer. Grey scroll bars automatically appear on the right and/or lower edge of the screen if the page contents are too big to fit into view.

search engine – A search engine is a web site you can use for finding something on the internet. The technology variously involves the use of 'bots' (search robots), spiders or crawlers. Popular search engines have developed into big web sites and information centres in their own right. Among the best known are AltaVista, Excite, Infoseek, Google, Lycos, Metasearch and Webcrawler.

secure sockets layer (SSL) – A standard piece of technology which ensures secure financial transactions and data flow over the internet.

server – Any computer on a network that provides access and serves information to other computers.

shareware – Software that you can try before you buy. Usually there is some kind of limitation such as an expiry date.

Shockwave – A popular piece of software produced by Macromedia, which enables you to view animations and other special effects on web sites.

signature file – This is a little text file in which you can place your address details, for adding to email and newsgroup messages.

smiley – A form of **emoticon**.

snail mail – The popular term for the standard postal service involving post-persons, vans, trains, planes, sacks and sorting offices.

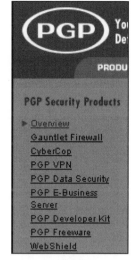

PGP Security Products
► Overview
 Gauntlet Firewall
 CyberCop
 PGP VPN
 PGP Data Security
 PGP E-Business Server
 PGP Developer Kit
 PGP Freeware
 WebShield

QuickTime™

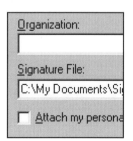

sniffer – A program on a computer system (usually an ISP's system) designed to collect information

spam – Electronic junk mail.

SSL – Secure socket layer, a key part of internet security technology.

subscribe – The term for accessing a newsgroup or internet mailing list in order to read and post messages.

surfing – Slang term for browsing the internet, especially following trails of links on pages across the world wide web.

TCP/IP – Transmission control protocol/internet protocol, the essential technology of the internet.

telnet – Software that allows you to connect via the internet to a remote computer and work as if you were a terminal linked to that system.

thread – An ongoing topic in a Usenet newsgroup or mailing list discussion. The term refers to the original message on a particular topic, and all the replies and other messages which spin off from it.

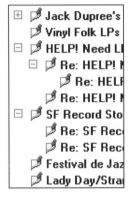

thumbnail – A small version of a graphic file which, when clicked, displays a larger version.

top level domain – The last piece of code in a domain name, such as .com or .uk

traffic – The amount of data flowing across the internet, to a particular web site, newsgroup or chat room, or as emails.

trojan horse – A program that seems to perform a useful task but is really a malevolent program designed to cause damage to a computer system.

UNIX – A computer operating system that has been in use for many years, mostly by larger systems.

uploading – The act of copying files from your PC to a server or other PC on the internet, for example when you are publishing your own web pages.

URL – Uniform resource locator, the address of each internet page. For instance the URL of Internet Handbooks is http://www.internet-handbooks.co.uk

Usenet – The collection of some 80,000 active newsgroups that make up a substantial part of the internet.

virtual reality – The presentation of a lifelike scenario in electronic form. It can be used for gaming, business or educational purposes.

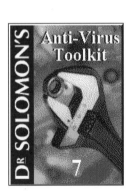

virus – A computer program maliciously designed to cause havoc to people's computer files.

web authoring – Creating HTML pages to upload onto the internet.

web – Short for the world wide web. See **WWW** below.

WAP – Wireless application protocol, new technology that enables mobile phones to access the internet.

webmaster Any person who manages a web site.

web rings – A network of interlinked web sites that share a common interest.

web site – A set of web pages, owned or managed by the same person or organisation, and which are interconnected by hyperlinks.

Windows – The operating system for personal computers developed by Bill Gates and the Microsoft Corporation. Windows 3.1 was followed by Windows 95, further enhanced by Windows 98. Windows 2000 is the latest.

wizard – A feature of many software programs that guides you through its main stages.

WWW – The world wide web. Since it began in 1994 this has become the most popular part of the internet. The web is now made up of more than a billion web pages of every imaginable description, typically linking to other pages.

WYSIWYG – 'What you see is what you get.' If you see it on the screen, then it should look just the same when you print it out.

Yahoo! – Probably the world's most popular internet directory and search engine.

Index

Index